DISCOVERING
VINTAGE
New Orleans

A Guide to the City's Timeless Shops, Bars, Hotels & More

BONNYE E. STUART
PHOTOGRAPHS BY LAURENCE P. STUART

Globe
Pequot

Guilford, Connecticut

All the information in this guidebook is subject to change. We recommend that you call ahead to obtain current information before traveling.

Globe Pequot

An imprint of Rowman & Littlefield

Distributed by NATIONAL BOOK NETWORK

Copyright © 2015 by Rowman & Littlefield

All photographs by Laurence P. Stuart unless otherwise noted

The Discovering Vintage series was created by Mitch Broder, the author of *Discovering Vintage New York: A Guide to the City's Timeless Shops, Bars, Delis & More.*

British Library Cataloguing in Publication Information Available

Library of Congress Cataloging-in-Publication Data

Stuart, Bonnye E.
  Discovering vintage New Orleans : a guide to the city's timeless shops, bars, hotels & more / Bonnye E. Stuart ; photos by Laurence P. Stuart. — First edition.
     pages cm
  Includes bibliographical references and index.
 ˙ISBN 978-1-4930-1265-7 (paperback) — ISBN 978-1-4930-1401-9 (e-book) 1. New Orleans (La.)—Guidebooks. 2. Stores, Retail—Louisiana—New Orleans—Guidebooks. 3. Restaurants—Louisiana—New Orleans—Guidebooks. 4. Theaters—Louisiana—New Orleans—Guidebooks. 5. Museums—Louisiana—New Orleans—Guidebooks. 6. Historic buildings—Louisiana—New Orleans—Guidebooks. 7. Historic sites—Louisiana—New Orleans—Guidebooks. I. Stuart, Laurence P. II. Title.
  F379.N53S78 2015
  917.63'350464—dc23
                          2015008344

⊗™ The paper used in this publication meets the minimum requirements of American National Standard for Information Sciences—Permanence of Paper for Printed Library Materials, ANSI/NISO Z39.48-1992.

Contents

Introduction ix

Andrew Jackson Hotel 1

Antoine's Restaurant 5

Audubon Butterfly Garden and Insectarium 10

Audubon Zoo 13

Aunt Sally's 19

Beauregard-Keyes House 24

Blaine Kern's Mardi Gras World 28

Bourbon French Parfums 32

Bud's Broiler 37

Camellia Grill 40

The Carousel Bar & Lounge 43

Cats Meow 47

City Park 50

The Columns Hotel 56

Commander's Palace 60

The Court of Two Sisters 65

The French Market 69

French Quarter Wedding Chapel 74

The Grocery 79

Hotel Villa Convento 83

House of Blues 87

Jackson Brewery Mall 91

Jackson Square 95

Joy Theater 100

Lafitte's Blacksmith Shop 104

La Pharmacie Française 107

Le Petit Théâtre du Vieux Carré. 110

Louis Armstrong Park 113

Louisiana's Civil War Museum 117

Mother-in-Law Lounge. 121

Mother's 124

Musée Conti Wax Museum. 128

New Canal Lighthouse Museum & Education Center . . . 131

New Orleans Historic Voodoo Museum. 135

Old Absinthe House 139

Old New Orleans Rum Distillery. 143

Our Lady of Guadalupe Church 148

Pat O'Brien's. 151

Preservation Hall 154

Rock 'n' Bowl 157

Rodrigue Studio. 160

Rubensteins 163

Saenger Theatre 168

Sazerac Bar & Grill 172

St. Augustine Church. .176

The St. Charles Avenue Streetcar 181

St. Louis Cemetery No. 1 & No. 2 184

St. Roch Cemetery and Shrine. 189

Steamboat *Natchez* Riverboat 193

The Superdome 198

Appendix A: Places by Category 202

Appendix B: Places by Neighborhood 205

Appendix C: Places by Year of Origin. 207

Bibliography 209

Index 212

About the Author

Bonnye Stuart is a ninth-generation New Orleans, Louisiana, native. She got her BA in advertising from the Manship School of Journalism at Louisiana State University and received her MA in communication from the University of New Orleans. She has been teaching at the university level for 26 years and at Winthrop University for 14 years. She teaches public relations, corporate communication, and international communication in the Department of Mass Communication. Before teaching she worked as a public relations professional for both for-profit and nonprofit organizations. She has had short stories, poems, and historically based stories and biographies published and has had several plays produced. She enjoys travel and viewing the world from various global perspectives. She has interviewed PR professionals in France, England, Greece, Thailand, and Singapore. Her research interests focus on the power of media images, specifically their early influence on the Troubles of Northern Ireland and role as agent for social change. She is married to Laurence P. Stuart, and they have four married children and 10 grandchildren.

Acknowledgments

Thanks go out to all the lovable characters in my personal New Orleans story. Without their support, this adventure could not have been completed. So here's a shout-out to children and spouses, David and Ruby, Elizabeth and Jeff, Jessica and Frank, and Christian and Jessica Lee. Tons of love go to grandchildren: Emily, Lauren, Jack, Tennyson, Braden, Lillian, Kingston, Logan, Elle, and Ariadne. Many other family members and friends added in no small way to my knowledge of New Orleans, but special gratitude for being so supportive of my book-writing experience goes to sisters Gloria and Gina. They won't hear it, but a loud "thank you" goes to all the people and places that added their tidbits to this tale of New Orleans, from websites, personal interviews, databases, archives, books, newspaper articles . . . I am fortunate to live in the Digital Age. Above all, I have to thank my husband, Laurence, for his help with this manuscript. Let me tell you why. He took all the photos for all the stories and that meant jumping out of the car on the I-10 expressway to get Xavier University, parking illegally along Baronne Street to capture The Roosevelt Hotel, walking hurriedly 8 blocks down Canal Street for the Rubensteins photo, waving off the eager valet service in front of The Columns Hotel, dealing with the inadequate low lighting of The Carousel Bar, talking his way past the hostess into The Court of Two Sisters, "recalculating" the GPS to find out-of-the-way places such as the Old New Orleans Rum Distillery and St. Augustine Church, and waiting patiently for St. Charles Avenue streetcars to pass each other at just the right time for that "perfect" picture. It also meant hours and hours in the car with me and our two dogs to get around the entire city, from the Mississippi River to Lake Pontchartrain, from Carrollton Avenue to Frenchmen Street, and to all the places in between on my "list of photos." Beyond this laudable feat, he also wrote a few of the stories and vintage spots and helped so much with the "fact finding" and "information organization" processes. And most of all, he made the experience of completing this book fun, from beginning to end! A last thank-you goes to Tracee Williams, my editor, who had the faith that I could get this book completed . . . and I did!

Introduction

New Orleans has flown flags of many nations, welcomed many cultures, and been called many names. "The Big Easy," "The City That Care Forgot," "The Crescent City," "America's Most Interesting City," "Hollywood South," and "The Northernmost Caribbean City" offers something extra, traditionally called lagniappe, for every visitor. You may already know something about this famous, or infamous, city, whether from Hurricane Katrina news coverage, friends who have attended the craziness of Mardi Gras or Jazz Fest, or listening to Arlo Guthrie's rendition of "City of New Orleans," a haunting song that you just can't get out of your head. But there's no substitute for experiencing New Orleans firsthand, up-close and personal!

This book will guide you around the city's many wonders as you explore the sights, sounds, and intrigues of a city with a very long history. Every street corner, every rickety, run-down building, every year in history has a tale to tell. If you listen very carefully, you can hear them all trying to share their stories of New Orleans with you.

As you saunter along Ursulines Street, the Hotel Villa Convento will try to convince you that it is the original House of the Rising Sun, the title of a beguiling song made famous by The Animals. Upstairs in Antoine's Restaurant, the Japanese Room, now open after being bolted shut for over four decades, wants to tell its story about the bombing at Pearl Harbor. The little mudbugs that locals call crawfish are anxious to lure you over to Mother's restaurant where you can "suck the heads" to experience an explosion of taste like none other. Other culinary delights are just waiting to welcome you to their New Orleans table of plenty. Try gulping down fresh salty oysters on the half shell at The French Market, devouring chili-smothered burgers and fries at Bud's Broiler by City Park, indulging in a sweet sugary praline from Aunt Sally's, or cooling off in the summer heat with a spearmint snowball with cream from Hansen's on Tchoupitoulas Street.

When you are in New Orleans, it's time to shake off any inhibitions you might have brought with you—walk, bike, or jump on a streetcar. Walking tours are plentiful. You can roam through stately homes, shudder through "haunted" tours, pick your way through above-ground cemetery vaults, or explore the inspirations of legendary writers, musicians, and artists. Bicycles are available in the French Quarter for long, leisurely tours of the old city and its adjacent historic areas. A jaunt up the magnificent St. Charles Avenue gives the stately mansions behind intricate wrought-iron fences a chance to tell their stories. Of course, the hundred-year-old oaks with remnants of Mardi Gras beads have a lot of tales to tell as well. With a day-pass, you can get off and on the streetcar to walk up Monkey Hill in Audubon Zoo, marvel at the architectural beauty of Tulane and Loyola Universities, or stop by The Grocery for a real po'boy. Make exploring New Orleans fun! Plan your forays by neighborhood, historic era, type of landmark . . . whatever you want! As you walk along antiques-laden Royal Street, bounce along on a horse-and-buggy tour, or lounge on 18th century–style velvet sofas in old French Quarter hotel bars to sip a mint julep or two, keep your eyes open and take in all that is uniquely New Orleans. Be sure to look for the little wall plaques on many old structures . . . someone famous has visited or some notable event has taken place right where you are standing!

New Orleans is my hometown. I am a ninth-generation descendant. I love the warmth of its people, the blending of the old and the new, the festivals and the concerts, the mixture of cuisines, the improbable legends, and the unbelievable truths. I hope you will love New Orleans too, and return often to visit this truly unique city.

ANDREW JACKSON HOTEL

919 ROYAL ST. • NEW ORLEANS, LA 70116 • (504) 561-5881

ANDREWJACKSONHOTEL.COM

You Can't Beat the Location

Where to stay when you visit the Crescent City? There are many great hotels, but if you want a little bit of history along with your bed-and-breakfast then you might consider the Andrew Jackson Hotel, a quaint historic European town house–style hotel. You can't miss the two-story building with its bright yellow façade and colonial blue shutters. Flags flying high above the street from the second-floor's intricately forged wrought-iron balcony announce the hotel's presence.

If you are looking for luxury, this is not the place for you. The building is very old and so are some of the furnishings. But if you want to be centrally located to everything in the Quarter and not pay a fortune, then give the Andrew Jackson a try. It is also a perfect place for a romantic getaway. What makes it so romantic? Besides being full of antique furnishings, high ceiling fans, and old southern charm, the hotel offers its signature "Silver Tray" in-room breakfast. For quiet, secluded nights, try booking one of the rooms that face the pool and the inner tropical courtyard. There are some second-story rooms with balconies that overlook the picturesque Creole courtyard area. If you want to be where the action is, then book one of the rooms with period French doors that open onto a balcony that stretches out over busy Royal Street. Here you can enjoy panoramic views of French Quarter life and spend some time people-watching both locals and tourists. There are some special rooms, called the King Balcony Suites. For the royal treatment, book one of these large suites with a separate living room and picturesque balcony where

you can relax, sip a mint julep, and soak up the sights and smells of the French Quarter. From the front steps of the Andrew Jackson you can get anywhere you want in the French Quarter very quickly. So if you are looking forward to shopping at the fantastic, treasure-laden, antiques stores along Royal Street, enjoying a shrimp po'boy at Acme Oyster House on Iberville Street, indulging in a Hurricane at Pat O'Brien's on St. Peter Street, or exploring the eclectic area around Jackson Square, you will be ever so close.

The Andrew Jackson Hotel is named, of course, after the hero of the War of 1812. Jackson is credited with saving New Orleans from British rule (even his conspiring with the pirate Jean Lafitte is celebrated) and his statue sits center stage in Jackson Square. The history of the site where the Andrew Jackson Hotel sits today goes back more than 200 years. The first historical record of a structure on this site was in the late 1700s when it was an all-boys orphanage and public school for the unfortunate children in a city plagued by disease, yellow fever, fire, and flood. The home for boys went up in flames in 1794 and the ashes were cleared to build the first permanent courthouse for the US District Court for the territory. It was here that the great Andrew Jackson appeared in court on an obstruction of justice charge levied against him for extending martial law after the war. Jackson refused to answer the accusation and promptly received a fine of $1,000, which he paid and then left the court. Outside the courthouse, Jackson spoke to a large crowd that had gathered shouting, "Vive le General Jackson!" His supporters raised the $1,000 to repay Jackson, but the general insisted the money be given to the widows and orphans of those who died in the Battle of New Orleans. In 1844, Congress ordered the fine to be repaid to Jackson with interest, in the amount of $2,700. The courthouse was torn down in 1888 to make way for a one-story boardinghouse, constructed with a colonial Spanish red-tiled roof and an inner courtyard, architectural motifs popular at the time. A second story was added later and this structure remains today as the 22-room Andrew Jackson Hotel, a quaint two-story brick complex surrounding a lush interior Creole courtyard.

In 1965, The Andrew Jackson French Quarter Hotel was listed on the National Register of Historic Places. The hotel has a distinct historic French Quarter character and is furnished with lovely 18th-century artifacts. It also has the distinction of being one of the most haunted hotels in the city and is on all the haunted tours. Next door to the left at 915 Royal is the famous wrought-iron "cornstalk" fence. This property was once owned by Judge Francois-Xavier Martin, who was appointed judge in February 1815 while the city was still under Jackson's martial law and later served as chief justice of the Louisiana Supreme Court. The structure you see today and its famous cornstalk fence was built after the judge sold the property. Today the Victorian home is a luxury boutique hotel. The beautiful cast-iron fence is made to resemble a row of cornstalks, with bursting ears of corn surrounded by intricate leaf-motifs. This hotel has attracted its share of celebrities including Bill and Hillary Clinton, and the King himself, Elvis Presley.

ANTOINE'S RESTAURANT

713 ST. LOUIS ST. • NEW ORLEANS, LA 70130

(504) 581-4422 • ANTOINES.COM

Fine Dining at Its World-Renowned Finest!

Visitors from around the world say eating at Antoine's Restaurant in the French Quarter is one of the most memorable culinary experiences of their lives. This exquisite, world-famous restaurant is steeped in history and its French Creole cuisine is described as "indescribable." Antoine's, the epitome of fine dining in New Orleans, is the original home of memorable epicurean creations such as Oysters Rockefeller, Pompano en Papillote, and Eggs Sardou.

When you enter the restaurant through the grand doorway street entrance, you will be escorted back in time. The beautiful, well-lighted, open room features many of the original 19th-century fixtures, including the sparkling chandeliers overhead. Through the French doors, just beyond the front room is the Large Annex, a room designed as a tribute to Antoine's wife, Julie. Most local families and businesses entertain their guests here and have had their own waiters for years.

There are numerous private dining areas; most are small, intimate spaces tucked away in corners both upstairs and downstairs. Three of the rooms are named after historical New Orleans Carnival krewes: the Rex Room, the Proteus Room, and the 12th Night Revelers Room. These festive rooms honor Mardi Gras royalty with photos of Carnival kings and queens and glass curio cabinets that exhibit glimmering tiaras, jeweled crowns, and sparkling scepters from well before most of you were born.

The Mystery Room got its name during the Prohibition era because the popular room was secreted away from the prying eyes of the law. To reach the room nestled at the end of a secluded hallway, you had to enter through the ladies' restroom. Here, alcohol was served in coffee cups, and if you were ever questioned as to what was in your cup, you were to say, "It's a mystery to me." The name Mystery Room has stuck to this day and the room is charmingly decorated with memorabilia from famous restaurants around the world.

The elegant salon atmosphere of the 1840 Room salutes a bygone era. Photographs of many generations of the founding Alciatore family hang on walls dressed luxuriously in rich, red decor. The Roy Alciatore Room, once called the Capitol Room because the antique wooden wall paneling came from the old Capitol building in Baton Rouge, and the Maison Verte Room are identical twins. Two sleek black marble fireplaces adorn each room and both share a second-floor balcony overlooking Rue St. Louis.

Cellars are not practical in New Orleans because the water table begins only a couple of inches below the surface. Therefore, Antoine's has what is best described as a "wine alley." The 165-foot-long and 7-foot-wide hallway, fed by a precise air-conditioning system, holds about 25,000 bottles of wine, which can be viewed by passersby on the sidewalk from a small window on Royal Street.

Antoine's Restaurant is a living museum, and if you get the chance to indulge in its culinary offerings, you can also arrange a tour of its dining rooms, bars, and wine cellar. But perhaps the most wondrous room of all is the Japanese Room. This space was originally designed with intricate Asian motifs and Oriental pieces. The walls and ceilings were painstakingly hand-painted with rich colors and Japanese patterns. It served as a large banquet room until the fateful day, December 7, 1941. On the day Pearl Harbor was bombed, Roy Louis Alciatore stormed up to the Japanese Room, bolted the door, and gave orders for it to remain locked indefinitely. Some say the room had not even been properly cleaned of table crumbs or chairs straightened, but no matter, no one was to go in, ever. Despite the lost revenue, the doors to the lavish room remained bolted for 43 years. The room was finally refurbished, and the hand-painted walls and ceilings were restored in 1984, using the artistic talents of many local artisans.

If you are ready to "pop the question," then you can book the Tabasco Room. This room is named after one of Antoine's most distinguished customers, Paul McIlhenny, of the famous Tabasco family. Of course, the room is painted Tabasco red, but its most distinguishing feature is that the room contains only one table, thus the perfect site for that once-in-a-lifetime, knee-bending occasion.

Through the years Antoine's has attracted famous guests such as Franklin Roosevelt, Herbert Hoover, the Duke and Duchess of Windsor, General Patton, Judy Garland, Bob Hope, Al Jolson, Carol Burnett, and Pope John II. Their recognizable photographs line the restaurant's walls.

Changes have come to Antoine's. The menu has been pared down and English translations of the traditional French Creole cuisine delicacies such as Crabes mous Amandine, Cerises jubilee, and Café Brûlot Diabolique have been added to the menu descriptions. A new Jazz Brunch is now offered on Sunday. Even the dress code has been relaxed. "We no longer enforce the coat and tie rule, but we still don't allow ripped jeans and flip-flops," says Yvonne Blount, fourth Alciatore generation, in a 2009 Associated Press article. "We very much feel a weight of responsibility," she adds.

You can make a reservation online. Antoine's is open Monday through Saturday, for lunch from 11:30 a.m. to 2 p.m. and for dinner from 5:30 to 9 p.m. Sunday Jazz Brunch is 11 a.m. to 2 p.m. Typical menu items include Huitres a la Foch, Crevettes remoulade, Pommes de terre brabant, Poulet aux champignons, and Crabes mous grilles. The food is somewhat pricey, but if you take the time to read about the history of the restaurant and spend some time walking around the various rooms and artifacts when you get there, you won't soon forget the combination of great food and New Orleans culture at Antoine's.

AUDUBON BUTTERFLY GARDEN AND INSECTARIUM

OLD NEW ORLEANS US CUSTOMS HOUSE • 423 CANAL ST.
NEW ORLEANS, LA • (504) 581-4629 / (800) 774-7394
AUDUBONINSTITUTE.ORG

Calling All Bug Lovers!

Whether you like touchy-feely relationships with creeping, crawling creatures or prefer to watch their activities behind thick plate glass, you will enjoy the time spent at the New Orleans Butterfly Garden and Insectarium, the largest free-standing bug museum in the United States. The gardens and insectarium opened in 2008 as part of the Audubon Park facilities and are run by the Audubon Nature Institute, a local nonprofit. The white marble–columned building in the 400 block of Canal Street houses over 900,000 species of insects in 23,000 square feet of space. Thousands of live insects, incredible mounted specimens, and interactive exhibits are available for the admission price of $16.50 for adults (13–64); $13 for seniors (65+); and $12 for children (2–12).

Trained experts and personnel are available to interpret the exhibits and guide visitors through a wondrous experience, up-close and personal. So put your fear in your pocket and venture boldly into the Insectarium. First stop—sit in an oversized "den" scaled as if you were a small bug. Look up, but don't be frightened by the large birds hovering overhead and spiders slowly inching toward you.

Not into feeling like a small lunch bite for giant birds and spiders? Then venture toward the Louisiana Swamp where you can examine closely, but in real size, spiders native to Louisiana habitats. This exhibit features life-size cypress trees and offers guided live animal encounters.

Not into arachnids? How about cockroaches? Move tentatively to the French Quarter street scene where you can visit some of the local insects such as Formosan subterranean termites, love bugs, mosquitoes, and cockroaches. For related activities, you can tune into the live "Cockroach Cam" online to see what the roaches do every minute of every day in a typical kitchen, or you can watch the "Roach-O-Vision movie," *Big Man on Campus* (1958) playing on the wall. Daily room cleaning and cockroach feeding takes place from 10:30 to 11 a.m., if you're interested!

Are elusive butterflies more your style? The Butterflies in Flight exhibit offers an amazing array of butterflies in a spectacular free-flight exhibit. Butterflies flutter and swirl through the Asian-inspired garden, resting on first one flower, and then the next, perhaps even on your shoulder for a brief second before they are off again. The Cooking Show and Cultural Café offer adventurous visitors unique dining experiences. An eclectic chef will introduce you to the culinary art of cooking with insects. You will even be offered a sample, if you think you can handle eating it!

This stop is also a great opportunity for you to see one of the most historic buildings in the country. The Insectarium is housed in the old US Custom House, a federal building begun in 1848 and built over a period of 33 years. The Treasury Department chose the design of Alexander Thompson Wood in 1847, but there would be a succession of eight architects before the building was completed. This monumental granite building was built to handle the increase in trade along the Mississippi River, which flowed through the booming port city of New Orleans. The first floor of a partially completed building was occupied by the US Customs Service (1856) and the Post Office (1860).

During the Civil War, a temporary roof was put on the unfinished building, which was used for the manufacture of gun carriages for the Confederacy, and when the Union took control of New Orleans, Union general Benjamin Butler captured the building and made it his headquarters. As many as 2,000 Confederate soldiers at a time were detained here during the war. Led by well-known architect Alfred B. Mullett, the Office of the Supervising Architect of the Treasury oversaw construction, which resumed in 1871. The building is notable for its Egyptian Revival columns, and the original arched brick ceiling in the Hall of Fame Gallery has been preserved. The grand Marble Hall has Corinthian columns exhibiting the heads of Mercury, the god of commerce, and Luna, the goddess who symbolizes New Orleans because her crescent-shaped brow seems to suggest the city's location in the bend of the Mississippi River. The building is listed on the National Register of Historic Places and received the National Historic Landmark designation in 1974.

But, let's get back to the bugs and the entomology museum. A Field Camp experience introduces you to the world of arthropods (animals that have segmented bodies and six or more jointed legs) and Life Underground shrinks you down to the size of the bugs, with oversized exhibition pieces, gigantic robotic insects, and a trap door spider surprise. In 2009, the museum received the award for Outstanding Achievement in a Science Center. From participating in "roach races" to watching butterflies emerge from cocoons to listening to lectures from field experts, there is something for everyone at the Butterfly Garden and Insectarium.

AUDUBON ZOO

6500 MAGAZINE ST. • NEW ORLEANS, LA 70118

(504) 581-4629 / (800) 774-7394 • AUDUBONINSTITUTE.ORG

Audubon Zoo: Unique Animals and a Long History!

Animals first inhabited the site now called Audubon Zoo during the 1884 World's Industrial and Cotton Centennial Exposition, which celebrated a hundred years of exporting cotton. Prominent figures were in attendance: John Philip Sousa, musician and band leader; Thomas Lipton, of Lipton tea fame; Julia Ward Howe, suffragette who resided over the Women's Exhibition; Mayor Joseph Guillotte; P. B. S. Pinchback, the first black acting governor of Louisiana; and others. The exposition was the largest US World Exposition to date and although it was not a financial success, over a million people attended the festivities.

Many animals were part of the Exposition. Buffalo Bill stunned fairgoers with his Wild West show and Indians rode through the streets on horses showing off their shooting skills. Extravaganza animal acts included donkeys, elk, and Texas Longhorns. When the fair was over, 58 acres of land were set aside as natural habitats for the animals left behind.

Today the 58-acre Audubon Zoo, home to more than 2,000 animals, consistently ranks high among the country's best zoos. Moss-laden live oaks, hundreds of years old, adorn the riverbank area along Magazine Street and many of the zoo facilities date back to the early 1900s. The zoo is part of the Audubon Nature Institute, named in honor of artist and naturalist John James Audubon, who lived in New Orleans in the 1800s. A statue of Audubon, high atop his pedestal, was created by Edward Virginius Valentine and unveiled

in a ceremony on November 26, 1910. The flight cage dates back to 1916 and the Odenheimer Sea Lion Pool with its graceful neo-classical columns was constructed in 1928. Art nouveau buildings and brick structures with bas-reliefs from the WPA era can be found throughout the grounds.

A day at Audubon Zoo will be an adventure to remember! Two of the zoo's most favorite animals are Asian elephants, Panya, 49, and Jean, 41. These beloved animals got new digs last year when they moved from their 1930s barn (990 square feet) where they had spent over three decades to a spacious 6,500-square-foot barn with heated, padded floors. The 42,000-square-foot Asian Domain habitat can accommodate up to four elephants, providing plenty of roaming room with gentle inclines, pools, shade trees, and a "fallen" tree enriched with natural pests for which the elephants can forage. But watch out! Part of the redesign of this enclosure includes the visitor-interactive opportunity for Panya and Jean to spray you with water from their trunks as they swim around their new 12-foot-deep pool.

In 1987, an alligator nest with 18 freshly hatched white alligator babies was discovered. The blue-eyed alligators with this mutation (leucism) received a lot of attention and quickly became a symbol

Vintage Spot
MONKEY HILL: EST. 1933

During the Great Depression, a project by the Civil Works Administration (CWA) involved digging a large lagoon to provide water for some of Audubon Zoo's exhibits such as the Swamp, Jungle and Pampas areas. During this project, as swamps were drained, workers slung the gooey mud onto a 40-foot mound, creating a "hill" that lay claim to being the highest point in New Orleans for over 50 years. Children in the area could not help climbing the hill and rolling down as "happy as a barrel of monkeys." In 1933, because of its popularity, the mound of mud was leveled at just over 27 feet and kept as a zoo attraction. A 1933 *Times-Picayune* article reported that "youngsters of New Orleans could run and boast that they had been on a real mountain." The name "Monkey Hill" stuck and it continues to provide a hilltop perch for the elevation-deprived children of New Orleans, a city that sits below sea level. A sign posted at Monkey Hill documents its purpose "to provide the children of this flat city with the experience of a hill," and continues, "If you climbed Monkey Hill 703 times, you will have climbed the equivalent of Mt. Kilimanjaro!"

Today Monkey Hill is a playground area for children, complete with waterfall, wading pool where tykes are encouraged to take off their shoes and cool their feet, rope net for climbing, and protective bronze lion sculptures. For years Monkey Hill was the highest point in the city, but a more recent "hill," the 53-foot-tall LaBorde Lookout in City Park, built from dirt removed in the construction of I-610 through New Orleans, now claims that title.

6500 Magazine St.; (504) 581-4629/(800) 774-7394; auduboninstitute.org

of the zoo's uniqueness. Other extraordinary attractions to look for are the rare white tiger King Zulu whose blue eyes survey all who enter his Audubon jungle and the endangered false gharial, a species of freshwater Southeast Asia crocodiles. False gharials are extremely hard to breed in captivity, but after years of cooperative effort with the Houston Zoo, two of the 20 eggs in a clutch hatched. The babies will grow to be 16 feet long.

Ready for lunch? You can stop at the Zoofari Café. While enjoying your meal you can still be part of the zoo experience. Newly mounted 46-inch LCD screens will entertain you with animal videos and interesting factoids about the zoo. After lunch you can experience hands-on animal encounters, educational programs, and exotic lush gardens.

Stroll through the award-winning Louisiana swamp exhibit and peer at local swamp critters such as nutrias, raccoons, and black bears and spy on the Cajun houseboat floating on the swampy waters where copperheads, blue crabs, and the world-famous white alligators live. The wild Jaguar Jungle and the natural habitat exhibit of the endangered whooping cranes should also be on your list. And don't forget the Reptile Encounter exhibit where you can visit the famous Komodo dragon, bearded lizard, green anaconda, and gaboon viper!

New Orleans is known for its hot, steamy days. You can ease the hot temperatures a bit at the Cool Zoo, a wild and wet water park. Youngsters can splash away at the jumping water spouts, alligator water slide, spider monkey soaker, and water-spitting snakes. There are three different splash zones for various ages, and parents can chill out too. Float leisurely down the Gator Run, a lazy-river attraction that includes two sandy beaches, or cool off in the shaded areas around the Snack N' Splash concession stand.

When you are finished with the zoo attractions, you can take a 7-mile Mississippi River cruise on the Riverboat *John James Audubon* from the zoo to the Aquarium of the Americas in the French Quarter. Soak up some more history of New Orleans and have a snack before your evening adventure begins.

Audubon Zoo is open Monday through Friday from 10 a.m. to 5 p.m. and Saturday and Sunday 10 a.m. to 6 p.m. The zoo is wheelchair accessible. Admission is $18.95 for adults (13–64); $14.95 for seniors (65+); $13.95 for children (2–12). So plan your trip to climb Monkey Hill, feed the alligators, or have lunch at the Zoofari Café!

AUNT SALLY'S

810 DECATUR ST. • 750 ST. CHARLES AVE.

NEW ORLEANS, LA 70116 • (800) 642-7257 • AUNTSALLYS.COM

Ready for a Sweet Treat?

J'm sure you've heard of the delicious pecan "pralines" to be found in abundance in New Orleans. Now it's time to indulge yourself. You have a choice of two locations for Aunt Sally's world-renowned pralines. So whether you are milling around the French Quarter or riding a streetcar uptown to Lee Circle, you are in easy reach of some delicious, mouthwatering pralines.

Pralines have been part of the city since horse-drawn carriages navigated the narrow cobblestone alleys and as much a part of the food culture of the old South as gumbo, jambalaya, and beignets. The praline recipe traveled from France where 18th-century French diplomat Cesar du Plessis-Praslin (pronounced "prah-lin") directed his chef, Clement Lassagne, to come up with a dessert that would use sugar-coated almonds. Louisiana settlers did not have access to French almonds or European beet sugar, so they turned to what they did have. Homegrown pecans (pronounced "puh-kahns" in the Crescent City) replaced the almonds and Louisiana sugar cane yielded the sweetness. In the New World "praslin" became "pralin" and today the Creole treat is known as a praline (still pronounced "prah-lin" no matter the spelling!). By the mid-1800s, successful entrepreneurial black women, called pralinieres, were peddling their sugary pralines on the streets of New Orleans. In his writings of early Louisiana, 18th-century historian Le Page du Pratz praised the pecan praline as one of the delicacies of New Orleans.

Aunt Sally's will capture your eye as you pass along the pavement, and you just *have* to watch the lady stirring the boiling copper pot.

Then the sweet smell from the bubbling concoction draws you irresistibly into the store, where you are offered free samples of the sugary discs with incredible buttery goodness. Aunt Sally's website says it all: "We proudly share our delicacy and deep roots with every person who wants to experience what we love and cherish—the most heavenly pralines you will ever taste." Debbie Hayne, working the counter, says, "Aunt Sally's is all about New Orleans! You have to try them!"

Aunt Sally's has been in the praline trade since 1935 when Pierre and Diane Bagur, New Orleans French Creoles, opened a small confectionery shop in Exchange Alley in the French Quarter before settling down on Decatur Street. Katie Walenter reports in a BestofNewOrleans.com article ("Aunt Sally's Pralines") that Pat McDonald Fowler, a Bagur granddaughter and Aunt Sally's merchandising and marketing consultant, says the shop quickly became "a destination for visitors who were intrigued by the romantic and mysterious French Quarter."

Today, Aunt Sally's has two locations. The more famous and beloved of tourists is its oldest location at 810 Decatur Street just down the street from the Café du Monde. This shop in the Historic French Market opened in 1940.

A second retail store and production facility opened in 2013 on 750 St. Charles Avenue along the streetcar line. Aunt Sally's completely restored a 1920s building in the Arts District neighborhood into a 10,000-square-foot, state-of-the-art praline-making facility. You can take a 1-hour tour and learn all about the history of pralines and some of the personalities from the shop's past. The tour includes a praline-making demonstration and a guided tasting tour through a variety of Aunt Sally's signature praline flavors.

At both locations, you can munch on samples and watch the Creole praline mixture being slowly cooked in open antique copper pots and then hand-poured one-by-one onto marble slabs. Aunt Sally's praline recipe is a closely guarded secret, passed down through four generations of the Bagur family and only known to the master praline makers who (as its website notes) "bring their skill and artistry to every batch of hand poured pralines."

Aunt Sally's also sells spices, condiments, jellies, muffuletta mixes, tubs of pralinettes, praline toppings, pecan pepper jellies, hot

sauces, and savory glazes in its unique gift store. Don't forget the log rolls! They are the best in town! You can also pick up souvenir books, posters, refrigerator magnets, and other knickknacks. If you don't want to tote your treasures home, you can order them online and have them shipped home to make the memories of your trip to New Orleans last longer.

Aunt Sally's has a wide range of types and flavors—classic Creole, creamy, chewy, lite, pralinettes, and more. The praline maker extraordinaire was featured on Food Network's *Kid in a Candy Store*. Host Adam Gertler checked out one of the creamy delicacies with a new twist, the Sugar and Spice praline with a hint of Tabasco sauce. A touch of the spicy zing from the McIlhenny Company of Avery Island's Tabasco Pepper Sauce is mixed with the sweet sugar cane praline, intertwining two Louisiana traditions for a unique explosion of taste.

Aunt Sally's has also partnered with local Kleinpeter Farms Dairy to supply the "praline" mixture for Bananas Foster Praline and Pralines & Cream ice creams. Are you hungry for some pralines yet?

Mixing up few ingredients might sound simple, but it's not easy. The sugar, pecans, and butter have to be added at just the right time in just the right amounts as the copper kettle rides over a gas flame. Two women tend to the roiling pot and get into a mixing and stirring rhythm. Then with years of practice behind them, they ladle out the hot confection to cool on the long marble counter. Ian McNulty writes in his January 8, 2014, *New Orleans Observer* article ("Candy Maker Expands but Keeps an Eye on Its Roots") that Fowler reminds those who think the process is easy that "the ingredients are straightforward. The hard thing is learning how to make it properly."

Aunt Sally's on Decatur is open 8 a.m. to 7 p.m. daily; the St. Charles store is open Monday through Friday from 7 a.m. to 5 p.m. and Saturday from 8 a.m. to 2 p.m.

The funny thing about getting a box of pralines . . . before you are halfway through the box you start to envision how pralines could make just about anything taste better . . . ice cream, pancakes, apple pie, peach cobbler—you get the picture!

BEAUREGARD-KEYES HOUSE

1113 CHARTRES ST. • NEW ORLEANS, LA 70116
(504) 523-7257 • BKHOUSE.ORG

Take a Step Back to a Different Time

ew Orleans is a very old city with tons of museums tucked here, there, and everywhere. But if you only have time for one "historic" museum, you might want to consider visiting the Beauregard-Keyes House, just across the street from the old Ursuline Convent in the French Quarter. This was a grand home during the golden age of New Orleans, an era that ended abruptly as the Civil War began claiming victims. Today the home echoes its former glory and gives insight into the lives of early citizens who shed their European mantle and began building a new American city. The architecture itself reflects the transition between the receding early 1800s Creole style and the emerging American style.

The Beauregard-Keyes House enjoys a rich legacy. It has been home to not one, but three, well-known local personalities. If you are a chess player, then you will recognize the name Paul Morphy. This New Orleans young man stunned the world with his chess-playing expertise, even at an early age, and he was born in this house in 1837. Are you a Civil War buff? General Pierre Gustave Toutant Beauregard, known as the "Creole Napoleon of the Civil War," returned to this house after the war ended. Perhaps you are an avid reader of life in old New Orleans. Frances Parkinson Keyes, novelist who preserved the splendor of the Crescent City in her novels, spent her last years here.

It is said that the Beauregard-Keyes House is one of the most haunted houses in the city. Are you a believer? Its ghostly occupants include Beauregard, an ambitious major fresh from the Mexican War

who moved into the Chartres Street house with his wife Caroline in 1860. President of the Confederacy Jefferson Davis sent Beauregard to South Carolina to give the order to fire on Fort Sumter, the action that officially started the Civil War. Beauregard, one of the most famous Confederate leaders, returned to an empty house at the end of the war; his beloved Caroline had died a year earlier. It seems Beauregard could not erase the memories of his loss at Shiloh and rumors spread that he roamed the halls at night in his uniform calling Caroline's name and attacking an invisible enemy. After the general died in 1893, people passing by the house claimed to hear a tired old voice repeating one word over and over: Shiloh. Witnesses (yes, witnesses . . . owners, neighbors, passersby, managers of the historic house, tour guides, ghost hunters) say they have seen the ballroom turn into a nightmare scene with weary soldiers standing deathly still while drums beat, rifle shots ring out, and men fall to the floor. Widespread ghoulish stories thwarted all local efforts to preserve the old home as a historic site.

By the early 1900s the house was owned by the Giacona family of wine merchants. The powerful Italian Mafia demanded protection money from the Giaconas, who upon refusal to pay turned the

Beauregard house into their fortress. One night in 1909, gunshots rang out and blood splattered the walls. In the end three Mafia thugs lay dead, their gushing blood running over the balcony to the ground below. Local newspapers reported the gun battle, making specific note of the large number of bullets found in the bodies. Some say gruesome screams can still be heard from the house, ringing out in the dead of night.

The house changed hands several times, slowly sinking into ruin, and in 1925, the new owner announced plans to build a macaroni factory on the property. The Beauregard Memorial Association was formed and raised funds to save Beauregard's house, even though most of the gardens would be demolished when the factory was built.

In 1944, Frances Parkinson Keyes, well-known novelist, rented the house and eventually acquired it and the corner property (the macaroni factory). While working on *Dinner at Antoine's*, *Chess Player*, and *Blue Camellia*, Keyes restored the house and gardens to their former glory. She founded the Keyes Foundation, which owns the home today. Magnolias, sculpted boxwoods, and an iron fountain adorn the brick-walled garden duplicating its original design. The home is full of period antiques and portraits of Beauregard. Keyes died in 1970 while living in the Beauregard House and her collection of antique dolls, teapots, fans, and fascinating folk costumes are on exhibit. "A Tea Party for the Dolls" is an annual children's event. Ghosts from this era include Keyes's beloved cocker spaniel, Lucky, who died just a few days after his mistress.

You will be welcomed to the historic Beauregard-Keyes House, on the list of National Historic Places, by docents in period costumes. Tours are on the hour, Monday through Saturday 10 a.m. to 3 p.m.

BLAINE KERN'S
MARDI GRAS WORLD

1380 PORT OF NEW ORLEANS PLACE • NEW ORLEANS, LA 70130

(504) 361-7821 / (800) 362-8213 • MARDIGRASWORLD.COM

Mr. Mardi Gras!

*J*f you are not one of the hundreds of thousands of the Mardi Gras faithful who pilgrimage from around the world to New Orleans to celebrate "Fat Tuesday," then your trip to the Big Easy would not be complete without a trip to the Blaine Kern Studios. Here you can get at least a visual impression of the mammoth colorful floats, some as long as 120 feet, that meander through the streets of New Orleans during Carnival season. These huge dazzling displays of artistry are pulled by tractors through frenzied crowds yelling "Throw me something, mister!"

Along the riverfront (you can grab a taxi or walk there in five minutes from the Convention Center) stands the Blaine Kern Studios, the self-acclaimed "world's biggest builder" of parade floats, and what a wonderful world it is!

The sheer size of the place is astounding. The floats, adorned with bright, colorful images sculpted in papier-mâché, flowers, feathers, wires, and glass beads to represent fantasy themes, take all year to produce. You may be surprised to learn that the floats are used for just one day a year . . . the day they roll through the streets of the city on their assigned parade routes.

The original mastermind behind all this glitz and glamour is a character that could have been scripted in a Disney movie. In fact, it was Walt Disney himself who inspired Blaine Kern to think beyond the commonly accepted style of Carnival floats. While the floats were artistic splendors, they were static and lifeless. Kern changed all of

that in the mid-1950s when he created a series of floats representing storybook characters and added moving heads and eyes that turned to gaze at the throngs of people in the streets below. The crowds' enthusiasm for the newly designed floats was so overwhelming that Blaine's reputation reached the ears of Walt Disney. After meeting Kern, Disney offered him a job in Los Angeles. But "The King of Mardi Gras," as Kern refers to himself, was dissuaded from leaving the city by his mentor, wealthy local businessman and captain of the prestigious Rex organization (founded in 1872), Darwin Fenner, who reportedly told him, "Son, let me tell you. You stay here in New Orleans; you're gonna be a big fish in a little pond. You go out there; you're gonna be a small fish in a big pond. Your fortune will be here in the future. Mardi Gras is democratizing; it's opening up to everybody."

Kern stayed and developed his craft. He visited Europe to study Carnival traditions in Cologne, Frankfurt, Nice, and Valencia. New Orleans Mardi Gras was changing. More krewes were organized to include everyday people, not just the elite, and parades began to roll through the suburbs of New Orleans. Mardi Gras became a celebration to be enjoyed by ordinary working class families.

And so, Kern's decision to stay in New Orleans paid off. The reportedly $20 million Kern holding company began to grow, creating

the magnificent Mardi Gras floats for a now seemingly endless number of Carnival season parades. Depending on when Shrove Tuesday falls in the calendar, parades can start rolling in neighborhoods throughout the city as early as late January. The sights of crews building reviewing stands along boulevards and pickup trucks toting home-built seats nailed to the top of ladders are the first signals that it's Mardi Gras season.

If you can't join the throngs of screaming people with outreached arms trying to catch a string of beads or a prized-possession doubloon during a Mardi Gras parade, then get on down to the Blaine Kern Studios. When you approach the entrance to "Mardi Gras World" (as Blaine Kern Studios are called), you are greeted by oversized heads of papier-mâché clowns, court jesters, and other character figures that flank the otherwise austere exterior. But once you enter the doorway, the magical world of make-believe comes to life with color, movement, and sound effects that will take your breath away. As you walk through the hallways of the whimsical exhibits, try to imagine that early in his career Kern was paid a mere $3,000 to paint ten floats for the Krewe of Alla. Now, Endymion, one of the largest of the float organizations, pays him up to $1.4 million for the design and creation of just one float! Today Blaine Kern Studios builds floats for over

40 parades a year, as well as provides innovative and breathtaking displays for theme parks such as Disney World, Universal Studios, Paramount Parks, Six Flags, and Japan's Toho Park. The studios have also taken on special projects at Harrah's, MGM Grand, and Circus casinos. Float-construction is a business, yes, but for the people of New Orleans Mardi Gras floats are local spectacles, enjoyed for free.

So, if the kids are with you, or if you still have a "kid" inside your heart, sign up for a 1-hour, spectacular tour of Mardi Gras magic on the riverfront at the Blaine Kern Studios. Enjoy dressing up in costumes, eating a slice of delicious King Cake (the official Mardi Gras delicacy, even out of season), and becoming part of a tradition that will never grow old. Tours are available seven days a week (except Thanksgiving, Christmas, Easter, and Mardi Gras) on the half hour from 9:30 a.m. to 4:30 p.m.

BOURBON FRENCH PARFUMS

805 ROYAL ST. • NEW ORLEANS, LA 70116

(504) 522-4480 • NEWORLEANSPERFUME.COM

The Sweet Smell of History

*T*ucked away behind a diminutive storefront in the old French Quarter is a perfumery that has been creating unique scents since 1843, not only for local patrons, but for lovers of customized perfumes around the world. Don't blink; you might miss the humble door and small picture window of wares that face a busy, often crowded, sidewalk. In an area that thrives on neon, you can look for the small, decorous sign hanging above the sidewalk as you saunter down Royal Street. If you go inside, Ms. Anne Hall will treat you like the old Creole aristocrats once served exclusively by the perfumery. She will offer you samples of various scents from the front counter display while she indulges in sharing a brief history of the business.

August Doussan arrived from France in 1843, and established the "Doussan French Perfumery" in the Vieux Carré. Doussan was the first full-time "parfumeur" in New Orleans and ran a lucrative business catering to the city's notable families. His skills of blending flowers and spices into marvelous parfums were renowned and his scents were in demand. One of his first fragrances was Kus Kus, a soft powdery spicy scent. It became an instant sensation and is still popular today. J. H. Tindel, a chemist who had studied the perfume trade in Europe, joined the business and together the two men developed a secret formula for a unique perfume called Eau de Cologne, a citrus blend later said to be Napoleon's favorite fragrance. New fragrances using local ingredients were added to the perfumery's offerings of traditional scents from Europe and Asia. When Doussan retired, Tindel changed the shop's name to the Bourbon French

Perfume Company. Tindel's expertise in chemistry led to the creation of new, exotic scents using Central and South American ingredients. The prosperous local business expanded as customers around the country and in Europe discovered the unique fragrances of the New Orleans perfumery. Marguerite Acker was brought on board to help customers while she learned the perfume business. It was quickly discovered that Acker had "le nez" (the nose), which allowed her to identify the ingredients in the perfumes just by taking a single whiff. Acker eventually bought the business and in 1973, her granddaughter, Alessandra Crain, inherited the Bourbon French Perfume Company. Crain also had "le nez" and she quickly began developing such unique scents as Voodoo Love, Marguerite Mon Idée, and Sans Nom. Today Mary Eleftorea Behlar owns the shop; she altered the name a little to Bourbon French Parfums. It is said she also has the gift of "le nez."

The perfumery prides itself on its tradition of developing new fragrances. Some of the newest scents include Sesquessence, created to celebrate Bourbon French Parfums' 150th year in business, La Pluie, the rain, and Eleftorea, Behlar's Greek name. A popular scent is Voodoo Love Cologne, a blend of voodoo high priestess Marie Laveau's love potions. It has been described as a dark, decadent, and mysterious blend with hints of cinnamon and amber.

The fragrances are displayed in old-fashioned glass cases and wooden cabinets. Delicious scents waft in from the fragrant blending room in the rear. This small shop on Royal Street continues to give personal attention to each and every one of its customers. A custom blend specialist is available to help you choose the essence that is right for you and your body chemistry. Then the specialist will design a fragrance for you that is as unique as you are. The methods used in creating fine fragrances have remained constant. At Bourbon French Parfums all blends are still mixed by hand in small batches and the scent is evaluated at every step of the process.

Men, don't worry. The perfumery has scents "Pour Femme" (for women) and "Pour Homme" (for men). So whether you want a special gift for the woman in your life, or you want your own individual cologne, you can indulge yourself here. The custom blend specialist will conduct a complete assessment of your body chemistry, your personality, your likes and dislikes, and then create your custom-blend formula which will be recorded and kept secret, for your use

Vintage Spot

M.S. RAU ANTIQUES: EST. 1912

As you leisurely stroll up and down Royal Street, you may be struck by the vast number of antiques and curio shops. They seem to stretch block after block. That's because New Orleans is a famous and well-known source for the unique and rare items sought by collectors and lovers of fine furniture, heirloom jewelry, and fine art.

M.S. Rau Antiques opened its doors for business in 1912 and today is reported to be the largest art and antiques gallery (in sales) in North America. Rau is owned by its original founding family who prides itself on educating customers on the value of investing in authentic collectibles that will increase in value, rather than buying cheap reproductions that will depreciate in value over time.

Shopping at this fine store is not for the faint of heart. Do not cross the Rau threshold if you are looking for bargain pricing. But if you want to step out of your comfort zone and make an investment for the future, walk on in and be dazzled by the splendor and beauty of the antiques inside. From large, grand-scale grandfather clocks to miniature music boxes, from 18th-century paintings to more "modern" sculptures, from Tiffany jewelry and heirloom sapphire rings to marble terrestrial globes, you will find everything you want. With obvious pride in what they do best, Rau's knowledgeable staff can help you navigate the packed showroom. Enjoy!

630 Royal St.; (888) 502-7009; rauantiques.com

only. Ms. Hall says, "We offer custom-blending and our customers' scents are theirs only." One customer remarked that although she hadn't been to the perfumery in many years, when she inquired about her specially crafted fragrance, the brown leather record book was taken out and her customized blend had been saved. She had her refill perfume within a few minutes.

You can order your scent in a variety of products such as perfume, cologne, eau de toilette, body lotion, bath gel, bath salts, or soap. Prices seem reasonable for such treasures. Soap is $6, a 4-ounce bottle of cologne is $34, body powder is $14, and ½ ounce of perfume is $52.50. Perfumes also come in handy travel sizes that are great for carry-on bags and take-home gifts. Full-size fragrances and gift sets, to be sent to your house, are packaged carefully and shipped promptly.

If you are going to New Orleans for a bachelorette party, you can book a "Blending Event" at the perfumery. The bride will receive 1 ounce of her customized perfume blend and attendees will get ¼ ounce of their own unique scents. Everyone gets a 4-ounce bag of bath salts. The cost is $300 for up to 10 attendees, but more guests can be accommodated for an additional $30 each.

The perfumery's website encourages everyone to "Come visit us at our Royal Street shop!" You can also get on the perfumery's mailing list to receive special announcements and event dates.

BUD'S BROILER

2800 VETERANS BLVD. (SEVEN LOCATIONS IN AND AROUND THE CITY) • KENNER, LA 70062 • (504) 466-0026 • BUDSBROILER.COM

This Bud's for You!

So, given that New Orleans is recognized as one of the most delightful, delectable, and desirous "food" cities in the world, why would you want to consider breaking down for a moment to try a burger and fries in a less than four-star restaurant?

Well, as the old folk song goes, "After you've been eating steak for a long time, beans, beans taste fine!"

Bud's Broiler is not only a New Orleans tradition, it's also a quick fix on the run for harried mothers with a car full of kids, construction workers looking for comfort food, hospital employees who want to run out and be back in less than 30 minutes, busy business executives who want to get away from the corporate milieu, and an energetic late-night crowd who need something to eat at 2 a.m.!

Started by Texas transplant Alfred "Bud" Saunders in 1952, the first Bud's Broiler restaurant opened in Metairie on the corner of Veterans Boulevard and Cleary Avenue in a unique A-frame building (pictured). We mention this location, not only because it was the first, but also because if you get off a plane at the New Orleans International Airport and are just famished, you can tell your taxi driver to head straight for Bud's at 2800 Veterans . . . he/she will no doubt know exactly where to stop and might even join you for a bite! When your cab pulls up to a rather shabby exterior, don't be alarmed . . . remember it's what's on the inside that counts.

What's so special about Bud's?

It's all in the way the charbroiled burger is cooked and the hickory sauce on top . . . created exclusively by Bud's Broiler. The ingredients are still a closely guarded secret.

When you try out this local hamburger joint (some would say New Orleans delicacy!), don't just order a burger with some stuff piled on it like you do at other fast-food restaurants . . . go for the gusto!

The posted menu board directs you to "Order by the Number." #1 is your basic burger with tomatoes, lettuce, etc., and fries, but as you work your way down the menu board you will find the delectable #4: burger, grated cheddar cheese, lettuce, tomatoes, pickles, onions, and chili, all topped with the special hickory sauce.

By the way, the menu board is only a guide for the novice. Those in the know walk straight up to the counter, start with a basic number, and then add or delete what they really want on their plate. For example, you can add onion rings or fries, or . . . you can blow your taste buds with smothered cheese fries.

The menu at Bud's has not changed much in the 60+ years it has been serving the people of New Orleans. You can also get hot dogs (with the same smothered choices), chicken, smoked sausage, nugget sandwiches, shrimp and catfish po'boys, and, to top the meal off, delicious, mouthwatering homemade desserts like apple, peach or cherry pies.

When you are deciding what to order to drink, go all the way and get a decadent strawberry or chocolate milk shake. Yep, it's got to be a milk shake if you want the total Bud's Broiler experience.

You can enjoy your meal while hanging out in a comfortable restaurant setting of multi-varnished, carved-into-many-times-over, wooden picnic tables, or if you are in a hurry, you can brown-bag the whole meal. Two of the locations are open 24 hours a day. If you are staying downtown, the most convenient location for you is across from City Park at 500 City Park Boulevard, a 10-minute cab ride. Be sure to check out City Park and all the activities available for you and the family if you get to this area.

No doubt, you will be all over the New Orleans area if you are staying longer than a couple of days, so make note of their other locations, such as in Harvey on the West Bank, on N. Causeway Boulevard across the street from the shopping center, at 3151 Calhoun Street near the Quarter, and on Jefferson Highway along the Mississippi River.

After Bud retired in 1980, his wife took over the running of the business for a while, and when she passed away in 1992, Bud's Broiler was purchased by Joseph Catalano, a longtime employee who had started his career with Bud's in 1962. Joe still works the counters and ensures that Bud's very friendly and loyal staff enforces its quality standards and customer satisfaction rules.

So, to answer the question: Why go looking for a burger in the Crescent City? Taste. You won't be able to forget the darn great taste, no matter how hard you try! We left the city some 20 years ago, after raising four children. Each was given the "Bud's Broiler" delectable rite of passage. To this day whenever we return for a visit, our saliva glands start working overtime about 60 miles from the city limits. Bud's Broiler is one of the first stops we make on the way to Aunt G's house. Of course, we indulge our palates and top off the meal with a piece of pie and a milk shake! (We don't tell Aunt G that's why we don't want any of her cookies, of course!)

Is your mouth watering yet? So is mine!

CAMELLIA GRILL

626 S. CARROLLTON AVE. • NEW ORLEANS, LA 70118

(504) 309-2679

Omelettes Have a "Secret" Ingredient

*L*ooking for the best omelette ever? It's time to get yourself down to the Camellia Grill, located in the Riverbend area, the point where Carrollton and St. Charles Avenues meet. You can take the historic St. Charles trolley to get there. From Canal Street, head away from the city (called downtown), go through the Garden District (called uptown) and when you reach the big bend in the Mississippi River you have arrived in Pigeontown (called P-town). P-town, once part of the City of Carrollton before it was annexed to New Orleans, is a fascinating mix of eclectic neighborhood businesses, shops, and restaurants. Pigeontown is not named after the bird, but rather after the broken English or "pidgin English" spoken in this area by resident immigrants. As a local explained, "When a whole neighborhood speaks pidgin English, you get Pigeontown."

The famous Camellia Grill is a diner-style eatery opened by the Schwartz family in 1946. From the outside the building looks like a miniature southern mansion. Inside, the grill is like a 1950s diner with countertop seating. Camellia Grill is a landmark spot in the city for many locals. It holds on tightly to its old-fashioned style, and vintage uniforms worn by waiters and waitresses famous for their prattle and personality inspire a retro feeling. Some say breakfast is the best meal to be had here, but others swear the grill's late night dining hours make after midnight the best time for a truly unique dining experience.

So what should you order? Let's start with the omelettes . . . that's spelled "omelette," not omelet. It's a French city, remember?

Enormous breakfast omelettes are served all day and night. The best of the best is the Chef's Special with turkey, bacon and ham, diced potatoes, and swiss cheese. One diner exclaimed that the Chef's Special was the "best omelette to ever touch my lips." The Chili omelette is great, too! It has chili over everything, including the fries. The Manhattan omelette and the Mexican omelette are pretty special, as well. You can't make a reservation at the Camellia Grill, and the line can sometimes extend out the door and down the block. But it moves pretty fast and there's lots of activity in the area to watch— that will make the time go by faster. Angela Furst, waiting her turn to get seated in the grill, disclosed that she knows the secret to the delicious omelettes. "The omelettes are the best and I think I know their secret," she said. But she wouldn't tell me that "secret." If you don't want to indulge in an exceptional omelette, you can order the pecan waffles. Also to die for! For lunch try a local delicacy: crispy, fried, not greasy, catfish. Be sure to pour on the Crystal hot sauce. The 10-inch deli roast beef po'boy, piled high with roast beef and gravy, is great too! Hickman's burger, a tasty choice, is topped with melted swiss cheese, sautéed mushrooms, and onions.

Camellia Grill is also known for its desserts. Late-night visitors come to top off their evening with something sweet and delicious.

The BETA chocolate pecan pie, heated on the grill, is often referred to as a slice of heaven. Many people go for the cheesecake, which has been described as "amazing." What you also need to know is that the grill serves its pies à la mode. But for the ultimate ice cream experience, try one of Camellia Grill's famous double-scoop freezes. Just do it—omelette, fries, chocolate freeze . . . and hot pecan pie!

Camellia Grill closed after Hurricane Katrina's visit to the Big Easy. When it failed to reopen the grill's front door was covered with hundreds of love notes begging it to open its doors soon. Restaurateur Hicham Khodr eventually bought the grill, extensively renovated the kitchen (but not the cherished dining room), and reopened in April of 2007 to mobs of hungry and thankful customers. This reopening of a New Orleans treasure was so celebrated that it made national news.

Camellia Grill remains as it always has: one brightly lit room with a high ceiling and a crenellated, marble-topped counter. Almost all the cooking goes on right behind the counter. Oh, and the linen napkins have returned. The grill serves red beans and rice only on Monday, as is the tradition in New Orleans, but on other days you can get the Mardi Gras sandwich of bacon, turkey, and corned beef. One patron described this treat as "a BLT that married a Reuben." The grill's fan base continues to extend across all generations of New Orleanians.

Camellia Grill is open 8 a.m. to 2 a.m.—you can get a meal here on most days, most holidays and after midnight. So there's no excuse not to enjoy at least one meal at the famous Camellia Grill during your stay in New Orleans.

THE CAROUSEL BAR & LOUNGE

214 ROYAL ST. • NEW ORLEANS, LA 70130

(504) 523-3341 • HOTELMONTELEONE.COM

A Circus Carousel for Adults

It's been turning for 65 years. Now it's your turn to take a spin, but you have to be at least 21 to ride this carousel! The Carousel Bar & Lounge at the Monteleone Hotel in the French Quarter is a favorite destination spot for both visitors and locals. The bar resembles a real-life carousel with bright lights, opulent filigree, and circus motifs. The colorful 25-seat merry-go-round bar sits center stage and the beautifully hand-painted barstools make a complete revolution every 15 minutes while patrons leisurely sip southern-style cocktails. Neworleans.com says the bar "revolves at a rate of about one cocktail per two rotations. Give or take." Don't worry, the 2,000 large, steel rollers turn slow enough that you won't fall off . . . or get nauseated.

There's lots of other comfy-chic seating in the lounge area, where you can sip pomegranate champagne cocktails while waiting for open seats at the Carousel, or if you feel you are not up for the revolving bar at all. Floor-to-ceiling windows overlook famed Royal Street and you can spend hours people-watching to your heart's content. This is the city's only revolving bar and its highly acclaimed live musical entertainment rolls on into the wee hours of the evening.

The hotel is family-owned and -operated. Its long history begins with an Italian immigrant, Antonio Monteleone, a proud Sicilian, who arrived in New Orleans around 1880. After setting up a cobbler shop on Royal Street, Antonio became a successful entrepreneur. In 1886, he bought the 64-room Commercial Hotel and then began buying more buildings. When the hotel became quite large, it was redesigned

in the flamboyant Beaux-Arts architectural style and its name was changed to the Hotel Monteleone. During the Great Depression, the Monteleone was the only hotel in the city to stay open. It was also the first hotel in New Orleans to treat guests to air-conditioning in its luxuriant lobby. By 1954, new dining and entertaining spaces with glittering chandeliers, polished marble floors, and gilded fixtures lured celebrities such as Liberace, Louis Prima, Etta James, and Nelson Eddy to its Swan Room nightclub. These were golden years for the Monteleone. Drinks such as the Goody and the Vieux Carré Cocktail were concocted here. Today the celebrated Hotel Monteleone is called the "Grand Dame of the French Quarter" and locals say the French Quarter begins at the lobby of the Monteleone.

The Monteleone was the home-away-from-home for several literary giants. Tennessee Williams wrote *The Rose Tattoo* while at the hotel and Ernest Hemingway mentions the Monteleone in "Night Before Battle." William Faulkner spent his honeymoon here in 1929, and also stayed here while he was writing *The Sound and the Fury*. Truman Capote did his share of writing while sitting in the Carousel Bar listening to live New Orleans jazz. You can stay in one of the rooms named in honor of these literary giants: the William Faulkner Suite, the Truman Capote Suite, the Tennessee Williams Suite, or the

Ernest Hemingway Penthouse Suite. More recently Anne Rice and John Grisham have stayed at the hotel. In 1999, the Hotel Monteleone joined an exclusive list of hotels in the country to receive the prestigious Literary Landmark designation.

Not into "literati"? How about ghosts? Ghosts roam freely through the Monteleone. The staff encourages guests to interact with the mostly friendly spirits. The Travel Channel's "Weird Travels" featured the otherworldly activities discovered by International Society for Paranormal Research investigators at the Hotel Monteleone on its program, *Spirits of the South*. The Monteleone has no thirteenth floor; the fourteenth floor comes after the twelfth floor. Films such as *Double Jeopardy* and several television programs have been filmed here.

But back to the Carousel Bar, where you're bound to feel like you are living the high life. Portraits of Jazz Era and Ziegfeld Follies icons from the 1920s and 1930s captivate patrons with their stunning intricate beadwork embellishments. In the plush, luxuriant surroundings you can order classic New Orleans drinks such as the Monteleone with Bulleit rye and orange bitters, the Criollo with Old New Orleans Cajun Spiced Rum, the Jezebel with Peychaud bitters, or the Roffignac, a Pierre Ferrand Ambre cognac cocktail named for an early 19th century New Orleans mayor. The bar is known for its Ramos Gin Fizz, one of the most iconic New Orleans drinks, named after Henry C. Ramos, owner of the now bygone Imperial Cabinet Saloon in downtown New Orleans. Its frothy combination of gin, heavy cream, syrup, fresh lemon juice, egg white, orange blossom water, and vanilla extract was invented in 1888 and called the New Orleans Fizz. The drink became instantly popular. History has it that when Louisiana governor Huey Long visited New York City in 1930, he flew a bartender up with him to teach the bartenders at the New Yorker Hotel how to properly mix the beloved Fizz so that he would never be without his favorite cocktail. This specialty drink requires a prep time of 10 to 15 minutes and considerable skill to perfect, so you can only get this cocktail in three or four sophisticated bars in the city.

"Bar Bites" in the Carousel can be just as exciting as imbibing the unique liquors. Indulge your palate with tasty culinary items such as Blue Crab & Crawfish Beignets, Monte Po Boys, Jambalaya, Crawfish

Pie and Filé Gumbo, BBQ ribs with Crystal Hot Sauce and braised collards, and "Frits" de Mer . . . catfish, Gulf shrimp, and oysters in a lemon dipping sauce. If you are hungry for more than bar food, the new Criollo Restaurant featuring contemporary Louisiana cuisine is located adjacent to the Carousel Bar.

Vogue Living named The Carousel Bar & Lounge one of 2014's Top Twenty Bars in the World. It is open 7 days a week from 11 a.m.— Until (as per its website).

CATS MEOW

701 BOURBON ST. • NEW ORLEANS, LA 70448

(504) 523-2788 • CATSKARAOKE.COM

No Dogs Allowed!

The Cats Meow is "the" place to exercise your lungs! Whether you can carry a tune or not, you will feel at home here. A reviewer on VirtualTourist.com describes Cats Meow as "loud, tacky . . . and definitely fun!" The karaoke bar sits unashamedly in the heart of the historic French Quarter where its vermilion paw prints on yellow walls beckon visitors from far and wide.

The bar is usually very crowded, which attests to its universal appeal. So if you think you are ready for *The Voice*, or even if you've been told you sing like a frightened cat this place is for you. You can belt out your favorite tunes, and the next morning your laryngitis will serve as a reminder of just how much fun you had at the Cats Meow. The bar has a great stage area where comical hosts keep the acts moving along, and in between the performances by singing imbibers, top-notch entertainers step up to the mike to entertain customers, in tune and on key. The bar has a great dance floor where everyone dances or just jumps up and down in the guise of dancing, and sings along. You can view the musical styles and more than 1,000 offerings online to plan your singing debut. You can also video your performance, and post it . . . if you want. If you are the quiet type, there's a lounge upstairs from which you can safely watch the goings-on in the energetic karaoke bar below.

There is no cover charge to get into the Cats Meow . . . so don't worry about wasting your money if you don't get discovered by an *American Idol* scout. The dress code is . . . well, just about anything goes. Some regulars suggest, "Wear what you want, be colorful and remember 'less is more' "!

Cats Meow has two great balconies from which you can see all the sights up and down Bourbon Street and people-watch to your heart's content. The Cats balconies are especially coveted spots during Mardi Gras when masked revelers fill the French Quarter's narrow streets. Just outside Cats Meow is the BourboCam, an EarthCam at the corner of Bourbon and St. Peter Streets. You can hang out on the street and become an instant Internet star. There's also a patio out back if you need to get away from all the "singing."

If you don't sing, but are looking for a place to act stupid, Cats Meow is still your place. Cats Meow has an affordable drink menu and potent drink specials. The "3 for 1 Happy Hour" special, a 32-ounce cocktail with three full shots, is available daily starting at 2 p.m. when bar business is slow. As the evening wears on, Cats Meow becomes crowded and by 11 p.m. the bar is rocking!

Here's a little history of the World Famous Cats Meow. The bar opened its doors in December 1989 when karaoke in America was just becoming popular. Cats was one of the first clubs to offer this new entertainment concept and in less than a year, Cats Meow became the largest "on premise" account for both Miller and Budweiser products in New Orleans. I guess that says something about the popularity of karaoke. If that's not enough to convince you, Pioneer, the audio company that made karaoke popular in the United States, once praised Cats Meow as "the BEST karaoke bar in the world."

Bourbon Street itself dates back to 1718 when it was called Rue Bourbon, after the French aristocratic House of Bourbon. The old structure that today houses Cats Meow was built around 1820 as a Creole town house with a Spanish-style cozy interior courtyard. The 19th-century architecture features dormer windows jutting out from the rooftop, French doors with period shutters, and two exterior balconies with wrought-iron railings that overlook Bourbon Street.

Entertainers, such as soul singer Seal and country artists Brooks and Dunn, have enjoyed some of the nightlife at Cats Meow. Other celebrities have frequented the bar: comedian/songwriter "Weird Al" Yankovic, Smashing Pumpkins, Depeche Mode, and NSYNC. Actors Tori Spelling and Mario Lopez have stopped in to sing, and software mogul Bill Gates of Microsoft also found his way to Cats Meow. Several television shows have shot episodes on-site at the club. The party atmosphere of Cats Meow has served as a festive backdrop for TV programs such as *The Regis and Kelly Show*, MTV's *Road Rules*, and *The Grind*. A song sung by basketball great Charles Barkley entertained the crowd and found its way onto YouTube. But getting more clicks than Barkley's performance was Miley Cyrus singing and twerking to "Baby Got Back." Check out youtube.com, if you dare!

"The magic spark that makes us the 'world's best karaoke bar' [is our] live mixing DJs and talented emcees," says the Cats website, adding, "The music is always a progressive mix of '50s through today's hits, classic rock, disco, dance, hip-hop, swing, and Top 40." The environment in Cats is fast-paced and energetic . . . and the music just keeps coming.

Cats Meow is famous for its wedding celebrations. Its Bachelorette package includes drink tickets, good for any drink, including the famous 32-ounce Hurricane, a Head Of The Line (HOTLine) pass to get on stage, clip-on cat tails in a variety of colors, headband-style cat ears, pink glow buttons with the Cats Meow "Ultimate Bachelorette Party" logo, a Cats Meow T-shirt for the bride (styles vary), and a DVD copy of bachelorettes' on-stage performances. Bachelors can get a fun package too, which includes souvenir glasses instead of cat tails and ears. Packages can be booked with a 3-day notice.

So, brush off your dancing shoes and straighten your ears, it's karaoke time in the Big Easy tonight!

CITY PARK

CITY PARK AND CARROLLTON AVE. • NEW ORLEANS, LA 70124

(504) 482-4888 • NEWORLEANSCITYPARK.COM

Need to Find Greener Pastures?

City Park is the place to breathe fresh air and soak up local color. At 1,500 acres, City Park is one of the ten largest urban parks in the country. It was once a swampy, oak-filled forest, home to Accolapissa and Biloxi Indians who carried on a vibrant trade along Bayou St. John. Later, the property was the site of the Allard Plantation, which passed into the hands of John McDonogh, who bequeathed it to the city upon his death. During the Great Depression, the Works Progress Administration spent over $12 million on City Park bridges, roadways, fountains, 10 miles of lagoons, a garden, and a stadium. More than 20,000 men and women were employed and all the work was done by hand. City Park offers a gumbo of activities for park visitors. Want to play tennis or golf? You can rent one of the 26 lighted tennis courts at the acclaimed Tennis Center or book a tee time at the 18-hole golf course that dates back to 1902 when it was one of only 80 courses in the country.

Need to feel the wind in your hair? Rent pedal boats or kayaks and cruise Big Lake with the ducks, geese, and swans. You can also rent a variety of bicycles: surrey, deuce coupe, chopper, quad sport, mountain, tandem, and others. The carousel (1906), one of only 100 antique wooden carousels still operating in the country, is a blast! Jump aboard a horse in flight (locals call them "flying horses" . . . and I remember begging to ride on the flying horses as a child), or if you are not so brave, hop on one of the standing horses or menagerie animals (giraffe, lion, camel), or sit in an oversized ornately gilded chariot. The carousel, listed on the National Register of Historic

Places, sat in 10 inches of water after Hurricane Katrina, but it's all restored now.

Interested in architecture? Various artistic styles from the turn of the century to modernity can be identified throughout the park. The little iron Storyteller Gazebo and the Spanish Mission–style Casino Building are two of the oldest structures in the park. Classical Greek

Vintage Spot
DUELING OAK: EST. 1854

Dueling was a considered the most chivalrous way to settle differences among the French population inhabiting New Orleans in the 1800s. The code duello outlined 26 rules for a proper duel, including time of day, weapon choice, and number of shots. It is said that more duels took place under the moss-laden Dueling Oaks at the foot of the Dreyfous Bridge in City Park than anywhere else. Here gentlemen in "affaires d'honneur" selected pistols, shotguns, sabers, or swords to uphold their reputations or protect their loved ones. Duels ended with the first drawing of blood. Early records show as many as 10 duels a day took place attracting upward of 200 spectators. Although dueling was outlawed in 1855, duels under the sprawling oaks continued until around 1890 when the practice simply died out as an acceptable method of dealing with personal insults. One of the historic oaks was lost in a 1949 hurricane, but the remaining Dueling Oak serves as a reminder of the city's intriguing history. The oak's unique marker, the last remaining hand-painted sign by park benefactor Mrs. Joy Luke, reads: "This site, history tells us was a favorite location for many duels fought by hot blooded young blades in the romantic antebellum era of the South. Here, mostly young French and Spanish gentlemen settled their differences with swords and pistols. This was the field of satisfaction for wounded pride and dishonor." The Dueling Oak can be found just to the left of the New Orleans Museum of Art (NOMA).

City Park; (504) 482-4888; neworleanscitypark.com

motifs, popular in early 20th century New Orleans, can be seen in the Popp Peristyle, an open-air pavilion, and the Popp Fountain. WPA-era sculptural elements can be seen in the hand-carved bas-reliefs on park bridges. Worth seeing is the 1936 McFadden Girl Scout Cabin donated to City Park by William Harding. Modern artworks also dot the City Park landscape.

Are you a flora enthusiast? You will be enthralled by the Botanical Garden and Conservatory, one of the finest existing examples of public garden designs dating from the WPA period. The 7-acre garden consists of several formal garden rooms and works by Enrique Alférez (1901–1999), a Mexican-born sculptor who lived in New Orleans. His *Shriever Fountain* (1932) with The Water Maiden stands in the center of the garden.

Are you a history buff? Tad Gormley Stadium, originally known as City Park Stadium, was built (1935-1936) by the WPA. Besides serving as a venue for local high school football teams, the stadium has hosted major events, such as the Catholic Church's Eighth National Eucharistic Congress in 1938, a concert by The Beatles in 1964 (called simply a "Beatles Show" in the City Park Board minutes), and the 1992 US Olympic Track & Field Trials. Gift shop guidebooks detail the locations and names of fountains, sculptures, bridges, and historical markers.

Looking for impressive sights? Alférez's *Popp Fountain* (1937) is a magnificent, 60-foot-wide fountain featuring underwater lighting and a cast bronze sculpture of leaping dolphins spraying water 30 feet into the air. The fountain is dramatically bordered by 26 wisteria-laden Corinthian columns. Several other fountains, dating from 1910 to 1961, and numerous old bridges, such as "Tickle Bridge," can be found throughout the park. Two impressive sights: the Monteleone Pillars (1914), 25-foot marble columns that mark the Esplanade Avenue entrance of City Park, and the Popp Bandstand, an architectural delight dedicated during a rare wartime festival in 1917.

Do you want to entertain the kiddos? Walk the nature trails of the 60-acre Couturie Forest and commune with countless trees, birds, and fish. Access the trail map online and hike up Laborde Mountain, the highest point in New Orleans at a staggering 43 feet above sea level. For the kid in you—a visit to Storyland is a must. More than

Vintage Spot

new ORLeans museum of aRT: est. 1911

If you are looking for fine arts in the Crescent City, then check out the New Orleans Museum of Art (NOMA) in City Park. This museum is the city's oldest fine arts institution and home to a permanent collection of 40,000 artworks, including works by Monet, Renoir, Picasso, Matisse, Pollock, and O'Keefe. NOMA also houses works by French impressionist Edgar Degas, who lived in New Orleans between 1871 and 1872 and painted several of his well-known pieces during his stay. You can also enjoy the museum's collections of photography, glass, ceramics, Faberge eggs, and Japanese paintings.

To the left of the museum you can stroll through the outdoor Sydney and Walda Besthoff Sculpture Garden of more than 60 sculptural works by world-renowned artists, valued at more than $25 million. Pieces such as the giant *Spider*, *Three People and Four Park Benches*, and *We Stand Together* are set amid the garden's 5 acres of footpaths and pedestrian bridges flanked by ancient live oaks draped in Spanish moss. The outdoor sculpture garden is open 7 days a week and is free. Audio tours are available, also free, and can be accessed on your cell phone. On the drive leading to the museum you can experience Molly Cochman's *Welcome* (2009), a cluster of grass mounds that spell "welcome" in Braille, installed as part of the Voodoo Music Experience festival.

1 Collins Diboll Circle; (504) 658-4100; NOMA.org

25 larger-than-life storybook sculptures serve as an imaginative playground. Storyland is a popular spot for birthday parties.

Just want to chill? Pack a picnic and squat under one of the 800-year-old live oaks, such as the McDonogh Oak (the oldest), or settle down at the Vixen Hill Gazebo just inside the entrance of the Carousel Garden Amusement Park. Another picturesque spot is the

Goldring/Woldenberg Great Lawn, with wide promenades bordered by 16-foot Medjool date palms, "swing arbors," and a unique water display where water runs off the roof in thin streams and flows into the fountain.

Don't like picnics? Want to be served your food? Then enjoy traditional southern-style cafe au lait and powdered beignets at Morning Call in the old Casino Building (1912). This former "cantina" (slurred by the Creole accent into "casino" and which continues to be called The Casino by locals) is an example of Spanish Mission Revival architecture. Gift shop, public restrooms, and Morning Call are open 24 hours a day, 7 days a week.

Whatever you like to do . . . there's something for you at City Park. There's no excuse not to plan a trip here because the park is accessible by foot, bus, streetcar, taxi, limo, automobile, bicycle, and even horse-drawn carriage.

THE COLUMNS HOTEL

3811 ST. CHARLES AVE. • NEW ORLEANS, LA 70115

504-899-9308 • THECOLUMNS.COM

Roll Back the Years, Roll Back the Centuries!

You can find The Columns Hotel on one of the most famous streets in New Orleans, St. Charles Avenue. This historic thoroughfare winds its way through the famed Garden District, an area settled by rich American merchants and businessmen who built homes here because they were not welcomed in the Creole neighborhoods in and around the French Quarter. At The Columns Hotel it is easy to sit back, relax, and drift back in time to days of floor-sweeping antebellum dresses, horse and buggy transportation, and southern-style mansions with their grand front galleries.

The Columns Hotel offers all this and more. The hotel lobby is full of elegant antique furniture, velvet couches, and Persian tapestries. A beautiful, old staircase leads to the rooms above the ground floor. But many more people, locals and tourists alike, come to The Columns, not for a hotel room, but to sit and leisurely sip mint juleps and Ramos Gin Fizzes in the warm evening breeze.

The hotel was originally the residential mansion of Simon Hernsheim, owner of the five-story La Belle Creole Cigar & Tobacco Factory that supplied all the major markets in Europe. Hernsheim employed more than a thousand men and women and produced 25 million tobacco products yearly. His was the largest factory in the city in the 1880s when New Orleans was fast becoming the tobacco center of the entire country. Business was so good that Hernsheim commissioned plans to be drawn by Thomas Sully for a palatial home on exclusive St. Charles Avenue. Sully, a New Orleans native, would become known locally as the king of architecture, designing more

homes on St. Charles Avenue than any other individual. Hernsheim's awesome Italianate chateau was known for its distinctive tower rising above the roof, arch-covered walkways, and luxurious spacious ballroom. In 1895 Simon lost both his wife, Ida, and his sister, Henrietta. Three years later his death was reported in the *New York Times*, which cited the cause of death as suicide by ingesting cyanide of potassium.

But Hernsheim's dream mansion has stood the test of time. The residence lost its signature tower forever to the 1915 Hurricane, but columns were added during the renovation, giving the current building its characteristic motif and namesake. In 1978, the controversial film *Pretty Baby*, with Brooke Shields, was filmed here, and when Jacques and Claire Creppel bought the hotel in 1980, they painstakingly restored it to its original grandeur. The Columns Hotel remains the only one of Sully's houses in the Italianate style still standing.

You can enjoy and be part of all this history. The rooms, from small and cozy to grand and spacious, occupy the top two floors of the hotel and are furnished with four-poster beds, antique armoires, charming fireplaces, and period bathtubs. On your way up the impressive mahogany staircase graced by antique murals notice how the sunburst stained-glass skylight floods the stairway. You get a complimentary full southern breakfast with your room and can even

Vintage Spot

CORNSTALK FENCE: EST. 1859

If you are uptown and want to catch a glimpse of a cornstalk fence (there are only three in the entire country) almost identical to the one around the Cornstalk Hotel in the French Quarter, then head over to the Garden District home built in 1859 for Colonel Robert Henry Short, a cotton merchant by trade. Short was a Kentucky native who opted to live in the "American" section of New Orleans like so many other English-speakers who did not feel welcome (and were definitely not welcomed) in the French Quarter. Colonel Short's villa, at the corner of Fourth and Prytania Streets, is an example of the early Italianate style made popular by architect Henry Howard. The house was occupied by the Yankee forces under Major General Nathaniel P. Banks during the Civil War and was returned to Short at the close of the war.

The fence was commissioned by Colonel Short, who was concerned about his wife's homesickness for her native Iowa. So to remind her of her cherished cornfields back home, Short ordered a wrought-iron fence that would resemble a row of cornstalks from Wood, Miltenberger, & Co., a company that cast many of New Orleans's most famous fences and balconies. This private residence is not open for tours, but the unique cornstalk fence can be viewed up close from the sidewalk.

1448 Fourth St.

call ahead to have room service deliver champagne and strawberries to your room upon check-in.

Even if you don't stay here, try to get to The Columns for happy hour, daily from 5 to 7 p.m., in the Victorian Lounge. This area resembles a traditional European pub with an exquisite bar of dark mahogany, antique fireplaces, and classic 15-foot ceilings. The Victorian Lounge was originally the family dining room and is known for its exquisite examples of Queen Anne design, such as the paneled ceiling of Honduras mahogany and the frescoed Greek-inspired frieze. This romantic setting of ageless elegance is enhanced by the original stained glass German chandelier still hanging in its place of honor. You can enjoy a traditional Pimm's Cup or a Sazerac Cocktail, whose pre–Civil War recipe was a New Orleans tradition earning the title of "official drink of the city." Celebrities Cameron Diaz, John Goodman, Michael Jordan, Clint Eastwood, Rod Stewart, Brooke Shields, and Harry Connick Jr. have all enjoyed a drink at this beautiful bar. It's an eclectic crowd that congregates here. You can raise your glass with tourists wearing beach shirts or uptown locals sporting tuxedos and evening wear. For a more intimate imbibing experience, there are several little rooms and patios tucked away where you can enjoy mint juleps, Brandy Milk Punch, Bloody Marys, or perhaps just a brewski!

You can also grab a meal in The Columns's opulent dining room, where overhead fans, bronze chandeliers, concave mirrors, Victorian decor, and French stained glass will transport you back in time. The dining room is open daily for breakfast and for Sunday Jazz Brunch from 11 a.m. to 3 p.m. The front porch Bistro, open daily and offering southern-style cuisine, is an outdoor dining room that overlooks the picturesque St. Charles Avenue trolley line. Hostess Candace Lightbourne says, "We have the best Bloody Marys in New Orleans, but everybody really raves about our Mint Juleps!"

The Columns Hotel, a European-style guest house drenched in old-world elegance, is on the National Register of Historic Places. The Columns is a popular spot to enjoy a drink or two and is in *Esquire*'s Guide to the 100 Best Bars in America. It also received nine awards in the Zagat 2007 Survey of New Orleans entertainment spots. What are you waiting for . . . jump on a streetcar and head to The Columns Hotel!

COMMANDER'S PALACE

1403 WASHINGTON AVE. • NEW ORLEANS, LA 70130

(504) 899-8221 • COMMANDERSPALACE.COM

Bread Pudding Soufflé . . . Delicious!

After the Louisiana Purchase, the "Americans" established themselves uptown in an area apart from and north of the French Quarter city center where French- and Spanish-speaking citizens lived. This section was called the City of Lafayette. Rich and powerful merchants, attracted by the growing trade of the region and supported by commercial interests along the Mississippi River, were buying property and building elaborate Greek Revival homes. Cotton agents, exporters, fur traders, and bankers flooded into this area called The Garden District because of its lush flora and beautiful tree-lined streets. The City of Lafayette grew rapidly and became part of New Orleans in 1852. By the 1860s, New Orleans was not only the largest cotton market in the world, it was also one of the wealthiest cities in the nation. But good times soon ended. The Civil War began and Louisiana seceded from the Union on January 26, 1861. A year later, New Orleans, a strategic port city, was occupied by Federal troops and all river traffic was controlled by the Union. The occupation was to last for a long and tragic 15 years.

But as the 19th century drew to a close, New Orleans was finally recovering from the harsh Yankee occupation and her people were settling into the routines and rituals of daily life. Trade flourished once again and entrepreneurs began looking for fresh opportunities to be of service to the new generation of wealthy businessmen.

In 1880, Emile Commander opened his restaurant on the corner of Washington Avenue and Coliseum Street just across from the new Lafayette Cemetery No. 1, the first planned cemetery in New

Orleans. The cemetery was an architectural masterpiece, laid out in 1833 by Benjamin Buisson, one of Napoleon's exiled lieutenants. Reflecting Buisson's influence, some of the streets in the area are named after Napoleon (Napoleon Avenue), his military victories (Milan, Constantinople, Marengo) and French cities associated with the "Little Corporal" (Lyon, Bordeau, Valence).

Commander's Palace, as Emile called his restaurant, was a stately Victorian clapboard mansion painted turquoise and white and featuring turrets, columns, and gingerbread motifs. Emile knew this would be a good location from which to provide sustenance to grieving families and friends before and after their visits to the gravesites. He wanted to appeal to the successful merchants settling in the area and serve the finest cuisine in an environment of utmost respectability. Emile decided against serving the traditional French fare so popular with the old New Orleans families. Instead, thinking the Americans would welcome a style of cooking that featured lots of seasonings, exotic spices, and a variety of peppers, he offered his guests Creole fare.

Commander's, as the restaurant is called by locals, was a success from the start. By the 1920s, a new management was continuing to offer the respectability of traditional dining in its first-floor dining

Vintage Spot

LAFAYETTE CEMETERY NO. 1: EST. 1833

This cemetery, bordered by Washington Avenue and Sixth, Prytania, and Coliseum Streets, was opened to serve the funeral needs of wealthy American businessmen and their families. Referred to as "Southern Yankees" by the Creole inhabitants of the city, these merchants moved into and opened successful businesses in the City of Lafayette, a suburb of New Orleans. Subsequently groups of working class immigrants, most notably from Germany and Ireland, started flooding into the adjacent area called the Irish Channel. You are welcome to walk around and discover some of the famous names on the above-ground vaults. Immigrants from 25 countries and natives of 26 states have been identified by the stone markers. You can spot "society tombs" of firefighter organizations, the Independent Order of Odd Fellows, the YMCA, the Home for Destitute Orphan Boys, and the New Orleans Home for Incurables. Try to locate the tomb of Judge Ferguson from the famous *Plessy v. Ferguson* Supreme Court "separate, but equal" case! Films such as *The Witching Hour*, *Double Jeopardy*, and *Dracula* used Lafayette Cemetery as backdrops. LeAnn Rimes and New Kids on the Block featured the cemetery in their music videos. About 7,000 people are buried in this 1-block area. The cemetery is open Monday through Friday from 8 a.m. to 2:30 p.m. and 8 a.m. to noon on Saturday. You can book the daily 10:30 a.m. walking tour of the cemetery on the website.

1400 Washington Ave.; (504) 525-3377;
saveourcemeteries.org

rooms, while providing space for illegal Roaring Twenties pastimes on its second floor. Riverboat captains and other less respectable clientele seeking these activities could enter the restaurant, unseen by the first-floor patrons, through a separate entrance. When Prohibition ended in 1933, Commander's once again reverted to what it knew best—providing a unique culinary experience of fine food and wine.

In 1944, Frank and Elinor Moran bought Commander's, renovated the building, and created menus with more contemporary cuisine. Twenty-five years later Commander's Palace found its way into the holdings of one of New Orleans's most famous restaurant families, the Brennans, who redesigned and modernized the interior that you see today. Large windows now overlook the lush inner courtyard, trellises with climbing vines bring the outdoors inside, and original paintings adorn the century-old walls. Commander's has been home to some of the most famous chefs in the world: Paul Prudhomme, father of blackened redfish, and Emeril Lagasse, television chef known for his culinary innovations and his call to "spice it up." Over its 135-year history Commander's has won too many awards to mention, but among the most recent are: *Southern Living*'s 2014 100 Best Restaurants in the South, Best of Show, Sweet, in The New Orleans Wine and Food Experience 2014, *Business Insider*'s The 45 Best Restaurants in America, and the #11 spot in the *Daily Meal*'s 101 Best Restaurants in America 2014. Manager Steve Woodruff says, "Commander's is the quintessential culinary experience. It's what dining in New Orleans is all about."

Today you can enjoy a unique dining experience at Commander's Palace. Take the St. Charles Avenue streetcar and get off just steps away from the restaurant. Commander's still serves Creole food but has added some contemporary food choices to its menu. Some of its signature dishes remain favorites, even for locals. Commander's traditional turtle soup takes three days to make. The dish is finished tableside with a flamboyant burst of aged sherry. This is a mouthwatering appetizer for $8.50 (I've had this soup many times; it is awesome!). Also featured on the menu are two-course lunch specials in the $17–$25 range. You can choose such delicacies as Louisiana Gumbo, West Indies Pickled Lobster and Avocado Salad, and Abita Barbecued Wild White Shrimp. If you ever get to Commander's, you have to try the Creole Bread Pudding Soufflé with warm whisky cream sauce for dessert—it is to die for! Looking for some libation? You can enjoy one of Commander's "best kept secrets"—25-cent martinis. There is a three-martini limit per person "'cause that's enough" as its menu states. The restaurant is open daily for lunch, dinner, and on Saturday and Sunday for a traditional Louisiana Jazz Brunch.

Commander's is an old New Orleans eatery that still enforces a dress code. Shorts and T-shirts are never allowed and you won't be seated if you are wearing sweats. Men can't wear flip-flops or open-toed sandals either. You can browse the gift area and bring home traditional pecan pralines, purchase a *Commander's Kitchen* cookbook with 150 recipes including Eggs Louis Armstrong and Braised Lamb Shanks with Merlot Mushroom Sauce, or buy *In the Land of Cocktails* with recipes for a sidecar, gin fizz, or Brandy Crusta.

THE COURT OF TWO SISTERS

613 ROYAL ST. • NEW ORLEANS, LA 70130

(504) 522-7261 • COURTOFTWOSISTERS.COM

Spice It Up with the Sisters!

Great romantic atmosphere and delicious Creole food! The servings are generous and the food is scrumptiously rich. The open air courtyard is gorgeous! That's what many loyal and returning patrons report. What will you say?

This property is steeped in history. The flamboyant Marquis de Vaudreuil, an early French governor who transformed the damp, marshy area into a cultural center called "Petit Paris," resided here. The second floor dining room is named the "Grand Marquis Room" in his honor. The 1832 city town house is named for two sisters, Emma and Bertha Camors, who had a shop on the ground floor facing the famed Royal Street. The sisters came into the picture in 1886 when Bertha, wife of the owner's son, and her sister opened a notions shop and called it "The Shop of Two Sisters." Their shop made Mardi Gras costumes and formal gowns and sold fine lace and perfume from France. They catered to the rich and prestigious families of the city and politely served tea and cake to customers in their beautiful and lush courtyard, said to be the largest in the city. The sisters died within 2 months of each other in 1944. They were 86 and 84 years old and are buried side by side in St. Louis Cemetery No. 3. After the notions shop closed, the space was a bistro, then a speakeasy. In 1963 it was bought by the Fein family, who began the painstaking task of restoring and preserving the building as The Court of Two Sisters restaurant. The sisters' tomb was also restored.

The entrance gates to The Court of Two Sisters were wrought in Spain. Legend has it that Queen Isabella had them blessed by the

65

FAMOUS
HISTORICAL
Court
OF
Two Sisters
RESTAURANT
SINCE 1832

Welcome

Catholic Church to imbue them with spiritual power—it's a tradition to touch the gates as you go in. The flags that you see as you enter are four of the ten sovereign flags that have flown over Louisiana and represent Spain, France, Louisiana, and the US. The wishing well in the courtyard is called the "Devil's Wishing Well" and it is said that Marie Laveau, who lived only a few blocks away, practiced voodoo rituals in the spacious torch-lit courtyard. The pirate Jean Lafitte is said to have killed three men in three separate duels under the courtyard's weeping willow tree . . . alas, Hurricane Betsy (1965) destroyed that willow tree. The 600 block of Royal Street is still referred to as "Governor's Row" because it has been home to five Louisiana governors. Two State Supreme Court justices, one future US Supreme Court justice, and President Zachary Taylor, before he was president, also resided in this prestigious area of Royal Street.

The restaurant has three dining rooms. The upstairs Marquis room has been described as comfortably shabby chic. Waiters are all in tails and there's always lots of fresh local seafood for the Oysters Bienville, Shrimp en Brochette, Corn Fried Des Allemands catfish, and Trout Meuniere. The turtle soup, a traditional New Orleans dish, is very good here. It is served thick and spicy with a dash of sherry for a wonderfully old world taste. Dessert choices include Doberge cake, Bananas Foster and, of course, the traditional bread pudding with whiskey sauce. There are lots of other delights; I mention these few just to wake up your taste buds. Chef Chad Penedo has been on the New Orleans food scene for a while. "I greatly enjoy sharing our traditional and original Creole dishes with locals and visitors from around the world," he says on the restaurant's website.

The best place to enjoy these tasty Creole dinners is in the sisters' picturesque open-air courtyard, which is lovely even during the winter. On hot days try to get seated under the cool canopy of spreading wisteria vines or near one of the bubbling fountains.

The Jazz Brunch is rated as one of the finest in the city, taking third place in *AAA Southern Traveler Magazine*'s list of best brunches in 2013. The jazz trio moves around the dining rooms and out to the spacious courtyard, so everyone gets a chance to enjoy the music. The Court of Two Sisters has received many other awards, including first place in the 2009 *Orleans Magazine* Reader's Choice competition for Best Place for Breakfast or Brunch and second

place for Best Outdoor Dining. Brunch is every day! You can choose from scrumptious foods such as omelettes stuffed with seasonal ingredients, jambalaya, shrimp étouffée, and boiled shrimp. Some say the $35 brunch is pricey, but you get to try all the traditional New Orleans dishes you were afraid to order at other restaurants . . . and you get a complimentary glass of the house Chardonnay, Cabernet Sauvignon, or champagne with your brunch.

The restaurant's website offers its menu in French, Spanish, German, Japanese, Italian, and Chinese, so there's no excuse not to prepare your palate for this culinary delight! Creole dinner is 5:30 to 10 p.m. every night.

Brunch is 9 a.m. to 3 p.m. and changes from breakfast to lunch selections. Dress is casual, but no tank tops, sleeveless shirts, or cut-off jeans are allowed.

If you will be in New Orleans during August, plan to take advantage of the COOLinary celebrations celebrating southern cuisine. Restaurants offer special COOLinary dinners and you can get a three-course meal of your choice of appetizer, entree, and dessert for a special COOLinary festival price. Some previous menu choices included crab ravigote, jumbo shrimp with caramelized onions, seafood étouffée, bread pudding, and chocolate mousse. You can call (800) 672-6124 for more information on the fest.

THE FRENCH MARKET

ALONG 1100 N. PETERS ST. • NEW ORLEANS, LA 70116

(504) 522-2621 • FRENCHMARKET.ORG

Let's "Make Groceries" at the French Market

Aaccording to Sally Reeves, author of *Making Groceries at the Old French Market* (a great read about the history of the market), "making groceries" is an old New Orleans expression that city residents traditionally used for food shopping. The expression derives from the French "faire son marché," which means "to do market shopping." But, the verb "faire" translates to English as "to make," thus "making groceries" was born in French colonial times and is an expression still used today by descendants of the oldest families in New Orleans.

The French Market at the end point of the French Quarter has been in business continuously for over 200 years. The open-air, covered market runs parallel to the river between Decatur and N. Peters Streets and is bordered at one end by Jackson Square and at the other by the old US Mint building. The French Market offers an array of merchandise from foodstuffs, locally made clothing, and imported trinkets from far-off lands to the latest technological gadgets. It is a 6-block flea market for bargain hunters with food vendor stalls, farmers' markets, and performances by brass bands and other local talent thrown in for lagniappe.

Evidence suggests that local Indian tribes used this area along the banks of the mighty Mississippi River as a place to trade food, tools, and crafts. As more and more settlers moved into the French Quarter, America's oldest market gradually grew from ramshackle lean-tos to what is today a cultural, commercial, and entertainment treasure. Ensuring a viable marketplace has not always been easy, and

Vintage Spot
FEELINGS CAFÉ: EST. 1979

Feelings Café is one of the most romantic restaurants in New Orleans. The restaurant and bar is in historic Faubourg Marigny, and way back in 1795, the structure was part of the Nicholas D'Aunoy plantation. The D'Aunoy plantation buildings included an "out" building, which is the present location of Feelings Café, and the slave quarters now houses the Patio Bar. Original fireplace bricks from the plantation have been recycled for the courtyard surface. Feelings is just a few blocks from the popular jazz clubs of Frenchmen Street.

The balcony of the upstairs dining room is a wine and cheese bar called Sentiments that features Marilyn Monroe and Elvis Presley memorabilia, including an Elvis clock with hips that swivel and the original Marilyn *Playboy* centerfold. From this vantage point you can gaze up at the stars or look below where patrons in the courtyard are enjoying the soft sounds from the piano bar. If you are in town on Thursday nights, you can take French classes while sipping your favorite cocktail.

The history and unique ambience of Feelings Café has been used for numerous commercials, television shows, music videos, and films. Feelings is open for dinner Tuesday through Saturday from 5:30 p.m. to 10:00 p.m The bar is open from 5 to 11 p.m., Tuesday through Saturday. On Sunday, brunch only is available from 11 a.m. to 3 p.m.

2600 Chartres St.; (504) 945-2222; feelingscafe.com

the market almost disappeared in the late 1890s due to neglect and lack of sanitation practices. But the dawn of the new century brought renewed interest from city leaders. During the Great Depression, with federal, state, local, and private funding, the market received a well-deserved face-lift, and the French Market Corporation was established to regulate, govern, and enforce standards of operation and growth opportunities. Many of the open-air buildings were in

disrepair with dangerous wiring systems. Many of these unfit, older buildings were demolished and a wholesale fish shed was added to cater to the growing demand for fresh gulf and lake fish, shrimp, oysters, and crawfish.

Today, the French Market has evolved into a viable organization that not only offers quality produce and licensed vendors, but which also hosts, educates, and entertains millions of locals and visitors each year. Return visitors believe the 2011 renovation project, which added cafe-style food venues and an entertainment stage, has helped revitalize the market. These small, comfy cafes offer countertop and tabletop seating areas where you can enjoy the unique flavors of southern and Cajun-style cooking while being entertained by some of the best local jazz entertainers and musical groups. During the year special events add to the excitement of visiting the French market. Try to make it to the Tomato Festival, the Latin American Food Festival, the Lighting of the Christmas Tree, or the Pumpkin Art show, all of which have become institutionalized city events drawing thousands of people. To find out what will be going on when you visit, go to the website or stop in at the French Market Visitor Center on the corner of Decatur and Dumaine Streets.

At the French Market you can purchase local offerings: sweet, sugary pralines, a bag of okra pods, snowballs, voodoo dolls, and plastic alligators. Of course, no list would be complete without the mention of coffee and the popular chicory additive. Just before you get to the market, you can stop at Café Du Monde for a cup of coffee and a portion of hot beignets smothered in powdered sugar. This open-air cafe, which has been in its current location since the 1860s, is a popular destination spot for social gatherings of late-night revelers, socialites, students, locals, tourists, and people of every nationality, speaking in a cacophony of accents.

If you are traveling to the Quarter by car, don't be deterred by thoughts of traffic or parking! Improvements on the Mississippi River side of the flood wall (just 100 feet from where you will be walking) have allowed for blocks-upon-blocks of parking. No car? Then just hop aboard the Riverfront streetcar and enjoy magnificent views of the Mississippi River and its bridges, steamboats, and ferries plowing across the muddy waters in the "crescent" bend of the river while making your way to the market. You can also stroll along the Moon Walk (the levee area named after Mayor Moon Landrieu) to reach the French Market and the Café Du Monde.

As you take in the unique sights, sounds, and aromas of the French Market, try to imagine that in the very place you are standing, an English, French, or Spanish visitor might also have stood to marvel at what historian Charles Lyell said in 1856, "stalls where hot coffee was selling in white china cups." It's a humbling, but joyous, experience.

FRENCH QUARTER WEDDING CHAPEL

333 BURGUNDY ST. • NEW ORLEANS, LA 70112

(504) 598-6808 • FRENCHQUARTERWEDDINGCHAPEL.COM

. . . Going to the Chapel of Love!

The Vieux Carré in old New Orleans is one of the most romantic spots on earth. Lush inner courtyards offer privacy from spying eyes, candlelit dinners promise intimate evenings, and the Mississippi River offers the chance to take quiet hand-holding strolls along the centuries-old riverbank. There are churches, synagogues, and hotels where many couples decide to tie the knot. They plan months, even years, in advance to book just the right venue, reserve the best band, and work out all the minute details of their most special day. BUT . . . there is only one wedding chapel in the French Quarter and you can get married there today!

The folks at the French Quarter Wedding Chapel are romantics at heart. The boutique chapel offers nondenominational wedding services as well as commitment ceremonies, vow renewals, and holy unions. The website promises to "make your wedding unforgettable" and can see you through the entire process from getting the marriage license to booking a horse and buggy to carry you off to a honeymoon suite. You can get married in the small chapel decorated in romantic grandeur, or your service can be held at other locations around town.

The small chapel on Burgundy in the French Quarter is painted a bright pink, making it stand out from the other businesses along the street. There's a little red scooter out front advertising the chapel. Reverend Tony Talavera, called Rev. Tony, is licensed by the State of Louisiana and the City of New Orleans to conduct marriage ceremonies. He and his wife, Lou Ann, bought the chapel when they

moved to New Orleans in 1999. Talavera co-founded The Louisiana Wedding Association in 2003. The chapel offers full-service wedding ceremonies. Lou Ann acts as staff photographer and coordinates "destination wedding" plans. Kristen Monnik, local violinist, plays sweetly and tenderly through the services.

The first thing you will notice when you enter the front door of the chapel is all the money hanging from the ceiling. The tradition started in 2001 when a bride was in a hurry to see her married name written out. She took a dollar bill from her new husband, signed her now-legal name, and told him to do the same. Then she gave the bill a kiss and handed it to Rev. Tony requesting it be hung from the 13-foot exposed cypress-beamed ceiling for all future brides to see. Today, among the multitude of antique lamps in the room, money from all over the world hangs from the chapel's ceiling. There are euros, pesos, and an Australian bill made out of plastic. Some couples desperate to seal their ceremony with a kiss and adorn the "money ceiling" have left alternative forms of currency, such as a maxed-out credit card, money orders, and personal checks. There is even an IOU! Try to find the "authentic" shrunken dollar bill (only in New Orleans) that's hanging somewhere from the money-strewn ceiling! Every bit of currency was sealed with a kiss from the loving couple before it was attached to the ceiling. It seems no one has ever asked for a dollar bill back, although many couples do return to say hello. Rev. Tony says he likes to believe that the loving kiss has stuck both the money to the ceiling and the couple to each other forever.

Ceremony prices start at $200 for the "Short Ceremony" of 20 minutes in the chapel, Monday through Thursday from 11 a.m. to 3 p.m. If you want to get married outdoors, the most popular spots are across from the St. Louis Cathedral, along the Mississippi River, in Audubon Park, in Washington Artillery Park across from Jackson Square, and at the entrance gates of the historic, and surprisingly picturesque, cemeteries around town. There are lots of options and wedding types, such as the "Carriage Wedding" for $655 that includes carriage rental, carriage driver, seating for the reverend, violinist, and photographer, and three additional guests. At the extreme end of your choices is a "New Orleans Wedding Flair Parade Ceremony" that includes a five-piece brass band, police escorts, and 25 white hankies

Vintage Spot
american Bicycle Rental company: est. 2010

The American Bicycle Rental Company is a local, family-owned, bike rental company in the French Quarter. It is located in a building that was once part of the old New Orleans Steel Products Company, and a couple of doors down from the French Quarter Wedding Chapel. Here you can rent one-speed, coaster-brake, American-made cruiser bicycles with comfortable 13-inch seats. The company does not rent mountain bikes; as its website notes, "New Orleans has neither mountains nor hills." You can also rent a kids' 20-inch BMX bike or a City Tandem cycle. You cannot reserve bikes; rentals are on a first-come, first-served basis. American Bicycle Rental has a large fleet of bikes, but they are much in demand on busy weekends and during festivals. The best time to secure a bike is between 9 and 11 a.m. You need to be 18 years of age or older (younger riders need a "release, waiver, and liability agreement" signed by a parent or legal guardian) to rent a bike and must present a valid ID and credit card. Don't worry—helmets, bike locks, and maps of the city are included in the rental price, but you can't get a baby seat nor a pull-behind child's carriage. You can also grab an ice-cold bottle of water from the fridge for $1.50 to take on the ride. You can rent by the hour on a sliding scale: the longer you rent the bicycle, the cheaper (per hour) it is. A 2-day rental is $65.

Why not take a 3-hour FreeWheelin' Bike Tour? It starts right at the bike rental's front door. Tour options are: "Creole & Crescent," "Mardi Gras, Mansions & Movie Stars," and "Wicked French Quarter" (at night). As you pedal off, tour guide Teddy promises that on his bike tours nothing will interfere with your view as you ride on your cool cruiser through the Quarter and to some of the historic spots beyond.

**325 Burgundy St.; (504) 324-8257;
bikerentalneworleans.com**

to wave during a traditional second-line procession. This option is $1,900 and you can use a credit card.

The French Quarter Wedding Chapel can work with you on all the details for your wedding. On its website you can find cake and bridal bouquet choices and price options. They can help with corsages, flower arrangements, limos, champagne (both alcoholic and non-alcoholic), unity candles, handfasting cords, second-line parasols, photographers, and more.

The French Quarter Wedding Chapel's mantra is "Weddings anytime, anywhere, 24 hours a day, 7 days a week." Rev. Tony strives to make his services unique and memorable, saying "Every wedding is special." Parker, a friend of my eldest son, surprised us all with his new bride. They had gotten married at the French Quarter Wedding Chapel. Parker said, "The day was wonderful and Rev. Tony was the best!"

You, too, can enjoy a "stress-free, beautiful, and entirely magical wedding experience" as the website promises and your first 30-minute consultation is free!

THE GROCERY

2854 ST. CHARLES AVE. • NEW ORLEANS, LA 70115

(504) 895-9524 • THEGROCERYNEWORLEANS.COM

Friendly and Funky

Jt's lunchtime. Are you ready for a real local food treat? From Canal Street, you can take the trolley down the famous St. Charles Avenue and get off on Sixth Street. The Grocery, a local sandwich shop, sits, half-hidden, on the corner under the oaks of St. Charles Avenue, between Sixth Street and Washington Avenue. Uptown and in the heart of the Garden District, the small, compact eatery is housed in a late 1800s building that once served the area as a pharmacy. The Garden District is a section of New Orleans that you must see. The area is chock full of southern-style mansions in one of the best-preserved areas in the country for 19th-century architecture. The area was given the name "Garden District" because its large, elegant homes were designed with extensive lush gardens and dense foliage. Also of note is the beautiful and intricate wrought-iron grillwork of gates, fences, balconies, and columns. After the French Quarter, this area is one of the most iconic representations of old New Orleans and is often featured in books, plays, and films. The entire area was declared a National Historic Landmark in 1974. The Grocery, immediately identifiable by its pink clapboard exterior, has been luring New Orleans regulars to this spot since 2003. The sign outside the front door announces that this establishment is not a grocery at all, stating "Not Really a Grocery Just Good Food."

This "not-really-a-grocery" is a little NOLA-style deli that features friendly service and tasty food. It touts itself as "The Home of the Pressed Po-Boy!" The interior dining area is festooned with flashy, eclectic artwork, and colorful adages on the walls. Note the "Miracles Can Happen" sign posted just below the sign: "If you get your food in

15 minutes it's a miracle!" (New Orleanians are known for their tongue-in-cheek sense of humor.) There's also a "Who dat?" decorated drum set hanging from the wall, adding to the eccentric decor.

So what should you order? There are many really good choices. The Grocery offers classic po'boys, chicken and sausage gumbo, and unique salads. Guests have applauded the Creole Corned Beef sandwich with provolone cheese, Russian dressing, and slaw, pressed to warm perfection. Others tout the muffuletta, a New Orleans traditional Italian sandwich, stuffed full of deli meats covered in gooey swiss cheese and layered with gobs of awesome diced olive salad. There's also a classic hot roast beef po'boy with gravy, horseradish mayonnaise, and jalapenos, or a hot pastrami po'boy on freshly baked Leidenheimer French bread. Try some Zapp's potato chips in a variety of flavors to go along with your sandwich. The smooth and steamy Brie and Mushroom Bisque is a great, thick soup to accompany your meal, or order some of the rich and meaty chicken and smoked sausage gumbo made Creole-style with a deep, dark roux and local seasonings and simmered for hours to create the perfect New Orleans gumbo.

Need more options? Try the pesto and chicken sandwich served on a pressed baguette or one of the daily specials such as the veggie melt with avocado and marinated tomatoes for those looking for a meatless sandwich. Then pick up a package of crab chips or a bag of Elmer's Chee-Weez and voilà, a unique, New Orleans–style lunch!

Want something light? The shrimp salad is great and the shrimp are plump and plentiful, or you can try the rocking grilled chicken salad with pecans, grapes, Parmesan cheese, and sundried tomato dressing. To end your eating explosion of taste, try the triple chocolate brownie. All delicacies are made in-house, not store-bought, and soups, salads, and sandwiches are made to order and from scratch!

Be warned! Do not go here for "fast food"! This is NOLA, after all, and food takes time to prepare. If you seem impatient, the people serving you will point out the sign about the miracle status of a 15-minute food delivery deadline. The sandwich makers are super friendly and will even help you select one of the local flavors of root beer to try. The Grocery has a refrigerator full of water, old-time sodas, bottled lemonades, local beers, and other goodies.

The Grocery offers great sandwiches, cheap beer, and local chips. What more could you want? You can eat inside where there are a

Vintage Spot

HANSEN'S SNO-BLIZ AND SWEETSHOP: EST. 1939

From March to October a ritualistic madness takes hold of many residents. It's all about a cup of ice with syrup poured over the top . . . or is it?

Snowballs (not to be confused with "snow cones" from other areas) are almost an art form in New Orleans. Blocks of ice are finely shaven powder-like snow . . . the finer the shavings, the more delicious the final product. But of equal importance is the quality and blending of the syrups, from the more mundane strawberry, chocolate, and vanilla, to nectar cream, satsuma, lemonade, spearmint, watermelon, nectarine, loganberry, root beer, cotton candy, and dare we say it, tutti frutti, just to name a few.

Hansen's is a family business, going back 75 years to when the current owner's grandparents started the business. Hansen's is recognized as one of the top five innovative and most delicious snowball experiences you will ever have (yes, there is a rating system for snowball stands)! When it is 95 degrees in the shade with 98 percent humidity, nothing beats a quick trip to Hansen's or one of the many other snowball stands throughout the city.

4801 Tchoupitoulas St.; (504) 891-9788; snobliz.com

few tables, or enjoy outdoor dining on the Avenue in nice weather. Another option is to take your beer and sandwich and do a walk-about. The staff can tell you about some nearby places of interest such as Lafayette Cemetery around the corner and The Columns Hotel just across St. Charles Avenue. If you need to catch the trolley back to your hotel, just ask inside and The Grocery staff will be happy to tell you where the closest streetcar stop is. Before you go, why not get a take-out order for supper—try the sausage melt of pork and alligator sausage, sautéed onions, roasted peppers, and provolone cheese. The Grocery is open for lunch Monday through Friday from 10 a.m. to 4 p.m. and on Saturday from 11 a.m. to 4 p.m.

HOTEL VILLA CONVENTO

616 URSULINES AVE. • NEW ORLEANS, LA 70116

(504) 522-1793 • VILLACONVENTO.COM

Your Mother Said Not to Go to the House of the Rising Sun

I'm sure you've heard the classic song, "The House of the Rising Sun," in which a young man laments wasting away his life "down in New Orleans" and admonishes mothers not to let their children spend their lives in "sin and misery." It's a sad song, and it speaks about a life no one would want. But perhaps the message is one we can all relate to on some level.

A recently excavated parcel of land may have been the site of the original House of the Rising Sun. Archaeologists say the remains of a 19th-century hotel unearthed on this site yielded items found in "bawdy" establishments, such as rouge pots and liquor bottles. This hotel, which opened for business in 1801, was the Rising Sun Hotel mentioned in an advertisement in the *Louisiana Gazette* on January 9, 1821, announcing that L.S. Hotchkiss and Co. had bought John Hull and Co.'s interests in the Rising Sun Hotel at 535 Conti St. The ad assured customers that the new owners would "maintain the character of giving the best entertainment, which this house has enjoyed for twenty years past." It further promised that "Gentlemen may here rely upon finding attentive Servants" and that "the bar will be supplied with genuine good Liquors. . . ." The Rising Sun Hotel was destroyed by fire in 1822.

Other history buffs point to an 1880s bordello operated by Madame Marianne Le Soleil (translation from French: The Sun) Levant at 828 St. Louis St. as the site of the bordello mentioned in the song. This beautifully restored house is not open to the public,

but the current owner did host Eric Burdon, singer for The Animals, who popularized the song in 1964. Burdon was supposedly in town researching the origins of the song.

But, if you want to say that you stayed at The House of the Rising Sun, then you have to believe the third option which suggests that the "House of the Rising Sun" is today Hotel Villa Convento at 616 Ursulines Avenue in the French Quarter. And this is your only chance to spend a night in the House of the Rising Sun—without the sin and misery, of course. It's a pretty ironic name considering the hotel's supposed reputation. "Convento" reflects the importance of religious orders in New Orleans and their houses called convents and its location on Ursulines Street underlines the esteem given to one particular New Orleans order of nuns—the Ursulines. This property was originally in possession of the Ursuline nuns who sold off part of their land to Jean Baptiste Poeyfarre for the construction of a Creole town house around 1833. Ten years later, his widow sold the property to Octave Voorheis. Voorheis lost the property around 1872, in the economic depression following the Civil War. In 1902, Pasquale Taromina purchased the property and his family lived here until 1946 when the home was turned into a boardinghouse. In 1981 Larry and Lela Campo purchased the property, restored the aging structure, and turned it into a cozy hotel. About the hotel's past, Manager Warren Campo said, "We know the hotel was a brothel at some point and there were a lot of visits by the police."

The Hotel Villa Convento is not one of the lavish hotels of New Orleans, but the small, 24-room Creole-style inn is full of southern charm. Gaslights flicker outside on the narrow French Quarter street. The small lobby of the hotel is graced by an elegant chandelier. Intricate wrought iron twists and turns around the balconies that overlook either the interior patio or Ursulines Street. All the rooms are decorated differently, and prices vary from $89 to $125 per room per night. Many rooms have interior natural brick walls, a design element that was popular during the mid 1800s. Each loft room on the third floor has a spiral staircase leading to the bedroom. Some rooms offer an antique four-poster queen bed with a period canopy. Breakfast is served in the courtyard garden, and includes traditional New Orleans coffee with chicory and fresh pastries from Le Croissant

d'Or, a popular patisserie across the street. Just about anything you could want to do in the French Quarter is within walking distance.

Some say that the hotel is haunted. If you hear children's laughter in the hall, you should be alarmed considering small children are not allowed to stay at the hotel. Some guests report being bothered by a mysterious madame knocking on doors as she makes her rounds. Some guests smell flowery perfume or feel their feet being tickled. One visitor reported, "I heard the most beautiful music from an old Victrola. . . . " One of the most prominent tenants when the hotel was the previous Old Town Villa boardinghouse was Jimmy Buffett, who returned years later with a film crew to shoot a documentary on his earlier life in New Orleans.

The Hotel Villa Convento is just 2 blocks north of the river and the French Market and 3 blocks east of Jackson Square. It's convenient, economical, and a great place to make friends, old and new.

HOUSE OF BLUES

225 DECATUR ST. • NEW ORLEANS, LA 70130

(504) 310-4999 • HOUSEOFBLUES.COM/NEWORLEANS

House of Blues in the Home of the Blues!

New Orleans is home to the Louisiana blues, a style that developed in the 1940s and 1950s and was founded on the rich blues roots of the city going back generations to Dixieland music. Buddy Bolden's band was playing blues before 1906 and the Original Dixieland Jazz Band's "Livery Stable Blues" is in this fast blues form. Influenced by jazz and Caribbean rhythms, the piano and saxophone are predominant instruments, but the guitar also contributes to the music. Local major figures of the genre include Professor Longhair, Guitar Slim, the most significant local blues guitarist in the post–World War II period, and Dr. John. New Orleans blues is generally cheerful and vocals range from smooth crooning to full-voiced gospel shouting.

So what could be more fun than attending a concert in a city that nurtured the blues? The first House of Blues was opened in Boston in 1992 (this venue closed in 2003) by Isaac Tigrett, co-founder of the Hard Rock Cafe, and Dan Aykroyd, co-star of the 1980 film *The Blues Brothers*. Their mission was to bring music of the rural South—blues, rhythm and blues, gospel, jazz, and rock 'n' roll—to northern ears. House of Blues venues, now across the country, pay homage to down home folk and the history of oppressed slaves. A metal box filled with mud from the Mississippi Delta is welded under every stage to keep the southern spirit beneath the feet of the performers, and unique stage curtains, taking over a thousand hours to create, reflect the struggles of the past. On its website the House of Blues explains, "Our 'Crazy Quilt' stage curtains pay respect to the enslaved Africans who used the Underground Railroad as a passage to freedom." House of Blues prides itself on its collection of Folk, Outsider, and Primitive artwork, pieces it calls the "Visual Blues." Currently, the House of Blues houses the largest collection of Outsider Art in the world.

The New Orleans House of Blues opened in 1994 and today is the longest-running venue of all 13 House of Blues establishments. At the entrance off an alley, you can see moss growing on the walls. The interior is subdued and lit with a soft blue light. The eclectic, juke joint decor is replete with hand-painted signs, posters, and folk art wall murals. Be sure to check out the bas-relief sculptures of famous artists on the ceiling.

The venue has two main concert areas: the Music Hall and the Parish. A smaller space, the outdoor Voodoo Garden, decorated with skulls, shrunken heads, and other voodoo motifs and painted in electric pink, is a great spot for local bands. Happy Hour is every Friday from 4 to 7 p.m. with free live blues music, and drink and appetizer specials! Big Mama's Lounge, a newly opened street-side bar, has an intimate bluesy atmosphere. There are bars both upstairs and downstairs, so don't worry, you won't have to wait long for your drink!

Music legends such as Fats Domino, the Neville Brothers, and Eric Clapton have performed at the House of Blues. On Sunday at 10 a.m., you can "raise the roof" at the new Gospel Brunch. Legendary gospel artist Kirk Franklin selects the talent and song list. Before and during the show you can enjoy an amazing all-you-can-eat buffet with southern specialty dishes, including the signature delicacy of chicken and waffles, and sip bottomless mimosas or imbibe at the Bloody Mary bar.

House of Blues New Orleans hosts the annual Brewsiana, a craft beer and music fest that brings together the best of southern Louisiana brewers, such as NOLA Brewery, Bayou Teche Biere, Chafunkta Brewing Co., Covington Brewhouse, Parish Brewing Co., Tin Roof Brewing Co., and Gnarly Barley Brewing Co., serving over 20 varieties of brews.

In 2014 Brad Pitt hosted a fundraiser for Make It Right, a foundation that builds homes in areas destroyed by Hurricane Katrina. Comedian Chris Rock was emcee and Bruno Mars and Kings of Leon performed

while Angelina Jolie, Sandra Bullock, and Sofia Vergara enjoyed the music. One guest was thrilled about catching the Neville Brothers playing to a standing-room-only crowd. Another fan was excited to join an impromptu sing-along with Ziggy Marley. One lucky patron reported catching Mardi Gras beads from Drew Carey, who showed up at the House of Blues during his stint as king of one of the Carnival krewes. Because the venue is intimate and small, bands often hang out after the show. One fan posted online that she "got to take pics with BALLYHOO!" The House of Blues offers acts you might not see in your hometown in a truly funky atmosphere with real southern hospitality. And you never know who you might run into here in the Big Easy House of Blues!

You can grab some really good food at the House of Blues restaurant, Crossroads. The new menu was created by celebrity chef and Food Network star, Aarón Sanchez. Appetizers include Cornbread with Maple Butter and Voodoo Shrimp simmered in an amber beer reduction on top of homemade jalapeño corn bread. Diners applaud the Applewood Bacon Wrapped Meatloaf and the "build your own burger" entrees. Superlative ratings go to the shrimp and grits dish with its alluring crispy fried grits cake. Jambalaya and andouille sausage and shrimp po'boys are also on the menu. And you

have to try the bread pudding! Lunch is Monday through Saturday from 11:30 a.m. to 4 p.m., and dinner is Sunday through Thursday from 4 to 10 p.m. and Friday and Saturday from 4 to 11 p.m.

Don't have the blues . . . enjoy the blues at the New Orleans House of Blues!

JACKSON BREWERY MALL

600 DECATUR ST. • NEW ORLEANS, LA 70130

(504) 566-7245 • JACKSONBREWERY.COM

The Jackson Brewery Is Not about Beer

ew Orleans was once a regional beer capital. City records from the late 19th century show there were about a dozen breweries in operation. The largest and most popular brands were Dixie, Regal, Falstaff, and Jax. These breweries would not survive the 20th century and the local brewing scene would move out of the city to St. Tammany Parish, on the north shore of Lake Pontchartrain.

The Dixie Brewing Company, founded in the Mid-City neighborhood of New Orleans in 1907, was devastated when Hurricane Katrina hit the city. The formidable brick building with its signature metal dome was flooded with 10 feet of rushing water. When the surge finally receded, looters hauled off everything of value, including the large copper distillation kettle. Today the brewery stands empty, and only the scarred walls remain to whisper tales of a once-vibrant business.

Regal beer was made by the American Brewing Company, which had bought a French Quarter winery in the 1800s. It survived Prohibition, just barely, and added Regal Ale, Regal Bock, and Toby Ale to its beer menu. The American Brewing Company closed in 1962 and the building was demolished to make way for the Royal Sonesta Hotel.

The Falstaff Brewing Corporation bought the National Brewery of New Orleans in 1937 and then closed this location on Gravier Street in 1979. The iconic building still bears a rooftop statue of beer's patron saint, King Gambrinus . . . and its Hurricane Katrina flood line. The building has recently been converted into apartments.

The Jackson Brewery on Decatur Street had the most prestigious location when it opened in 1890. Designed and constructed by German-born and -trained architect Dietrich Einsiedel, the brewery became a focal point of New Orleans beer culture. As the largest independent brewery in the South and the 10th largest single-plant brewery in the country, it employed 500 workers and produced 350,000 to 450,000 barrels of Jax beer a year. The brewery fell on hard times in the late 1970s.

The brewery was closed, but its location along the Mississippi River in the historic French Quarter saved the iconic building. In 1984, the Jackson Brewery structure was extensively renovated to open as the Jax Brewery mall.

Today you can't see any brewing, but you can drink the beer. The brewery is now a four-story mall with more than 50 stores and eateries. There are several bars and restaurants for your drinking pleasure and lots of unique dining places such as the Lazy River, which serves local cuisine in a beautiful dining room and southern-style terrace that look out over spectacular vistas of the French Quarter and Mississippi River. Food court options are Hotsy's Grill, New Orleans Fried Chicken, C's Seafood & Subs, JAX Daiquiri Café, and many others. Visitors say they like the food court's inexpensive

Vintage Spot

nola brewery: est. 2008

If you really want to visit an operating brewery and savor a local beer brewed in the New Orleans city limits, you are in luck! Your venture to the renovated old warehouse on Tchoupitoulas Street in the old Irish Channel neighborhood that houses the young NOLA Brewery will be well rewarded. NOLA's taproom is ultramodern with its long bar and tall wooden tables and stools. You can catch football games and other popular sporting events on the giant TV screens. The taproom employs a 16-tap system to give patrons a wide selection of beers from traditional to specialty brews. You can test unique brews that include fresh herbs and fruits in their ingredients. Just Peach is a blonde ale with fresh-squeezed peach juice, Girl Scout Cookie is a creative blend of Irish Channel Stout with mint, and the NOLA Brown favorite combines English dark ale with the sweetness of chocolate, coffee, and caramel. NOLA's taproom is open Monday and Wednesday through Friday from 2 p.m. to until and on weekends from 11 a.m. to until. You can also get a meal to go with your brew from the on-site La Cocinta and Rue Chow food trucks. Taproom prices range from $3 to $4 for a 10-ounce serving and $5 to $7 per 16-ounce pint. Tours of the brewery are available on Friday beginning at 2 p.m. The admission price of $5 includes a brewery tour and souvenir pint glass. The taproom is expanding to twice the current size and will soon fill two stories of another old adjacent building. A grill will also serve bar food. So get on down there!

3001 Tchoupitoulas St.; (404) 375-3732; nolabrewing.com

meals and being able to relax while looking out across the river. You can see riverboats leisurely plowing the muddy waters and watch visitors who stroll along the Moon Walk or sit on the grassy riverbank entranced by Old Man River. Of course, there are bars in the food court too where you can order some of the local beer varieties, such as Abita beer (the choice of many locals), and the ales and lagers from a newcomer, the NOLA Brewing Company.

And you can shop, shop, shop. Specialty shops include the Big Easy T-Shirt Company, Gumbo Kids, Cajun Clothing by Perlis, Destination New Orleans, Home Team Sportswear, Orleans Jewels, Mardi Gras Parade, and tons more. There are some of the traditional mall shops too.

The Jax Art Gallery offers posters, prints, postcards, and local artwork, and you can have your purchases custom-framed for you. Street Scene carries limited edition hand-painted woodgraphs of New Orleans scenes. These make wonderful unique gifts from the Crescent City. Pick up some bottles of locally made hot sauces, Jackson Square refrigerator magnets, fleur-de-lis key chains, or alligator eggs to bring home to the kids. Every store in The Shops at Jax Brewery offers tax-free shopping for international visitors. Louisiana is the only state in the US that offers this shopping benefit.

If you want to learn a little about the history of the Jackson Brewery, you can visit the Jax Collection on the second floor of the mall. This small, free museum preserves the glory days of the New Orleans Jackson Brewery. Check out the original Jax beer cans, bottles, and signature bar signs. There are some animated vintage commercials you can watch too.

Worth the trip is a visit to the third floor of the mall where you will find the "Louisiana's Living Treasures" exhibit. This is a replica of a typical Cajun village. You will be treated to displays and demonstrations.

As you plan your day in the French Quarter, be sure to put Jax Brewery on your to-do list. You'll find lots to do and lots to see!

JACKSON SQUARE

HEART OF THE FRENCH QUARTER
NEW ORLEANS, LA 70116 • (504) 658-3200
EXPERIENCENEWORLEANS.COM/JACKSON-SQUARE.HTML

It Might Be "Square" to Say It,
But Jackson's Got It All

*J*ackson Square, the epicenter and heart of New Orleans, that is. If you ask nine out of ten visitors to the Big Easy what they saw and where they visited, the first thing they will try to describe is Jackson Square. This wonderfully picturesque and vibrant 2.5 acres of the city is rich in history, bustling in commerce, and downright fun!

You can start your day at Jackson Square early in the morning and enjoy fresh beignets and coffee at the famous Café Du Monde. The coffee is served "au lait" and the hot beignets are lavishly sprinkled with powdered sugar. Then you can stroll through the crowded French Market stalls, shop for unique gifts, sample distinctive foods, listen to the street musicians, or sit along the wrought-iron fence around the square while some of the most talented artists in the world paint your portrait or sketch a caricature of you with a bloated head and diminished body parts!

With many, many restaurants and cafes in and around the square, you will never go hungry. And if you have a mind to learn something, there are walking tours, carriage tours, bike tours, and self-guided tours where you can absorb every imaginable piece of historical fact and fiction about the area.

Jackson Square, originally named by the French who founded the city as the Place d'Armes, has been the gathering place for city residents since the days of its settlement in 1718. It has served as a meeting place for both joyous and gut-wrenching occasions. Public offenders were humiliated in stocks, and murderers were executed there.

In 2005, President Bush stood on the steps leading to the mighty Mississippi River and tried to give hope to the hundreds of thousands of local residents stranded during the aftermath of Hurricane Katrina. World-famous dignitaries and just plain ordinary folk have stepped out into Jackson Square from the doors of the St. Louis Cathedral after praying on a Sunday morning. Newly married couples and their guests have marched in second-line processions past the Cabildo (house of government) and down into the streets of the French Quarter.

Although Andrew Jackson himself laid the original cornerstone to his monument in 1840, the square was not officially renamed in his honor until 1851, and his statue that stands center-stage was not completed until 1855. When Jackson Square's makeover was nearly complete, the wrought-iron fence that still surrounds the Square today was installed and the pathways were laid out in their current configuration. This work did not always go smoothly, but finally all construction was complete. As plans were made to dedicate the statue on January 8, 1856, the 41st anniversary of the Battle of New

Vintage Spot

MOON WALK: EST. 1976

In 1976 a promenade was constructed along the Mississippi River from which you can view the river's daily activities. Climb the stairs near the Café Du Monde, stroll through Washington Artillery Park, cross the train tracks, and walk a few steps to the river's bank. The small Washington Artillery Park has a real Civil War cannon and was built to honor the 141st Field Artillery of the Louisiana National Guard founded in 1838. This plaza has great views of the St. Louis Cathedral, the Cabildo, and the mighty Mississippi River, and thanks to a constant breeze you will feel a little cooler than you did walking the sultry city streets of the French Quarter. The Moon Walk, a mile-long stretch along the levee, is a great place for po'boy picnics, or you can rest idly on one of the iron park benches to people-watch or boat-spot. There's lots of bustling activity to view as the port of New Orleans is one of the largest ports in the US and river traffic includes historic paddle steamers, huge container vessels, and cruise ships. The Moon Walk features some public art and is a popular place for street performers and jazz musicians. The annual spring French Quarter Festival uses this scenic boardwalk as a music venue and this spot is much in demand for viewing July 4 fireworks during the festivities known as "Go Fourth on the River." The Moon Walk project was named for the mayor of New Orleans at the time of its construction, "Moon" Landrieu.

Opposite Jackson Square, next to Jackson Brewery

Orleans, another obstacle raised its ugly head. *The Southerner*, the ship carrying the statue from Baltimore, Maryland, where it had been made, was delayed due to weather for more than a month. The statue was finally unveiled on February 9.

Even after installation, further controversies ensued. Union troops captured the city of New Orleans in 1862, and General Benjamin

Butler, upset by the disrespect for his troops shown by local citizens, spitefully carved into the granite sides of the base: "The Union must and shall be preserved." Other mishaps occurred, with Jackson's head falling to the ground while boys climbed on the statue in 1934 and his sword being stolen in 1960 (never found, but replaced).

But the square, statue, and gardens do not begin to tell the whole story of this wonderful area that will take hours to explore. You can visit the St. Louis Cathedral, whose spire magnificently rises to the sky and which forms the iconic postcard backdrop if you are viewing the Square from the river's built-up levee. The Cabildo next door is home to a comprehensive museum of Louisiana's history. In 1803 the Louisiana Purchase was finalized there and Louisiana officially became part of the US. After the signing ceremony, the Stars and Stripes were raised over the Place d'Armes. Adjacent to the cathedral you can find the Presbytere, which features exhibits such as "Living with Hurricanes: Katrina and Beyond" and "Mardi Gras: It's Carnival Time in Louisiana."

Wherever you are in the area, you must look up above the shops and appreciate the Lower and Upper Pontalba Apartments, flanking both sides of the square. You will be viewing the oldest apartment buildings in the United States. The complex of retail shops at ground level and the prestigious apartments above were created more than two centuries ago by Baroness Micaela de Pontalba, partly as a business investment, but more as a tribute to her late father, who had a vision of a city plaza with retail space and living quarters situated as two symmetrical wings to a central temple (the cathedral).

So, whether it is winter, spring, summer, or fall, mild cool breezes or 90 percent humidity, Jackson Square has much to offer. Make sure you reserve enough time to fully explore this sparkling gem in the crown of the French Quarter.

JOY THEATER

1200 CANAL ST. • NEW ORLEANS, LA 70112
504-528-9569 • THEJOYTHEATER.COM

There's Nothing Quite as Grand as an Old-Fashioned Movie House

For nearly two centuries Canal Street has been the heart of commerce in New Orleans and the surrounding Gulf Coast region. In the early days the thriving business district lured merchants, traders, bankers, politicians, and entrepreneurs. The French, Spanish, Creole, and eventually the Americans all helped establish the downtown area. Back in the last century, New Orleanians flocked to Canal Street as the premier place to work, play, and shop. Whether they worked downtown or took the bus to get there, they shopped at the grand department stores of Maison Blanche, Rubensteins, and D. H. Holmes, perused the scandalous boutiques in the French Quarter, and looked forward to catching a picture show at the Joy Theater, simply referred to as The Joy. This theater was a favorite meeting place long before the small, neon-less, children-laden neighborhood theaters began to spring up.

According to the theater's website, Joy Theater was the first movie palace to be constructed in New Orleans after the Depression ended and the wartime ban on new construction was lifted. It was designed by Favrot and Reed, a long-standing, renowned Louisiana architectural firm with numerous buildings on the National Register of Historic Places today. The Joy was built on the southwest corner of Canal Street and Elks Place and was completed in late 1946. Its lavish construction reflected the new optimism of city businesses following the end of World War II. It became one of four large movie theaters that were built in downtown New Orleans. The years 1946–1948 saw

a substantial rise in movie theater attendance, and New Orleans residents flocked to its first-run movies. The Joy was acclaimed as a "modern" theater because of its huge neon marquee and art deco architecture and, according to its website, "is one of the few remaining examples of the post-war movie palace in New Orleans." The Joy's 1940s art deco grandeur still makes a bold statement in the downtown area. The shining, shimmering marquee reflects the opulence of what once was the finest movie house of its time. Its grandiose presence is punctuated by an iconic neon sign that beckons to patrons.

I remember Saturdays during my teen years waiting impatiently at the nearest bus stop to my house in Gentilly where I could catch a bus for seven cents and head downtown. I would meet my cousin Pam in front of D. H. Holmes and cross the busy Canal Street to buy our tickets from the little old lady behind the plate-glass window of the ticket rotunda set in front of the theater. Then we would enter the cool, air-conditioned interior, purchase a drink and a huge pickle, and head for the perfect seat, near the front, of course. The adrenaline rush of being able to see a first-run movie was pure joy.

The theater ran its first feature film, *Lover Come Back*, starring Lucille Ball and George Brent, on February 7, 1947. The theater's longest-running film was *Jaws*, which ran for 20 weeks in 1975. Lines to get into the theater often extended well down the block; *Come September* with Sandra Dee and Rock Hudson had gaggles of girls in lines stretching around the corner. Blockbuster movies like *Godzilla* promised spectacular viewing and the creature itself roamed the lobby running up the aisles making small children scream in terror. More recently *Late Night with David Letterman* was broadcast from the theater in a "held over" show. You can see a ton of nostalgic old photos on the theater's website. Eventually the glory days ended due to competition from multi-screen, stadium-seating film venues that were all the rage in suburbia by the late 1900s. In 2003 The Joy's marquee went dark and the heavy glass doors were sealed and locked.

Today the Joy Theater, after a $5 million renovation, is a historic landmark. The state-of-the-art venue with high-tech sound and lighting systems lures live music concerts, theatrical performances, comedy shows, and special events to its stage. The Joy boasts that it offers an "intimate" experience for patrons with its booking of small Broadway and off-Broadway shows. The website says, "The Joy Theater is dedicated to bringing 'joy' back to the City of New Orleans." You too can enjoy the glitz and glamour that once belonged only to the exquisite movie houses of the past.

Even if you don't get to see a production, just standing in front of The Joy and looking up at the huge glittering marquee will take you back in time! The 11,000-square-foot masonry and steel building has 8,500 square feet at the main level and can seat 1,200 guests. There is also seating in the 2,500-square-foot space at the upper mezzanine and balcony levels. The building symbolizes the vibrant historic legacy of downtown New Orleans and it lives on in the minds of generations of New Orleanians who fondly remember the vibrancy of Canal Street. The theater is within walking distance of the French Quarter, or you can take a Canal Street streetcar that runs down the tracks in the center of the wide boulevard, or you can hop on a St. Charles trolley from the uptown areas and Garden District and head to Canal Street.

LAFITTE'S BLACKSMITH SHOP

941 BOURBON ST. • NEW ORLEANS, LA 70116
(504) 593-9761 • LAFITTESBLACKSMITHSHOP.COM

Ahoy, Ye Mates! Here's a Place to Pass a Good Time!

Ready to relax, kick off your shoes, and experience New Orleans as it was in its earliest beginnings? The city was founded when Jean-Baptiste Le Moyne de Bienville arrived in 1718 in what is the present-day French Quarter with 80 convicted salt smugglers and began to clear the land. Lafitte's Blacksmith Shop is one of the first buildings in the city and is reputed to be the oldest structure used as a bar in the entire US. What a great place to travel back in time to the days when New Orleans was a favored resting spot for trappers, merchants, plantation owners, and . . . cunning pirates!

So what makes this old building unique? When you arrive at the bar, one of the first things you'll see is the briquette-entre-poteaux style of construction. Now, you may not know this architectural term, but you can't help notice the outside walls of soft Louisiana-made mud bricks set between wooden posts, and then covered with a plaster facade. This style was an import from the sugar plantations on the French colony of Saint-Domingue (later Haiti). The original circa 1722 building, constructed just after the founding of the city, was destroyed, but the present building used the same French Colonial style in the reconstruction 50 years later. And a 1772 construction date is nothing to laugh at!

But what you might find even more fascinating is that this building is believed to have been used by the Lafitte Brothers, Jean and Pierre, as the base for their Barataria smuggling operation between 1772 and 1791. The legend is based on records that show the property was

owned by the family of Simon Duroche, aka Castillon, who was an adventurer and entrepreneur, and the wily privateer Captain Rene Beluche, commander of the *Spy*, one of the 100 ships in Lafitte's fleet.

As you sip a potent Hurricane in the small bar on the corner of Bourbon and St. Phillip Streets, you can just imagine the Lafitte brothers passing stolen goods to eager agents and wealthy citizens in the city. Records show that by 1808 the brothers had a lucrative, though nefarious, business as smugglers and slave importers. Their band of cutthroats attacked incoming ships navigating the Gulf of Mexico south of New Orleans and used the small blacksmith shop on Bourbon Street to disperse their plunder of liquor, weapons, gold, and slaves.

Eventually, the government shut down Lafitte's operation. The brothers and their men were arrested. But Jean Lafitte met personally with Andrew Jackson and agreed to help fight the British in the Battle of New Orleans in 1815 in exchange for pardons. Jean Lafitte was hailed as a patriot and proclaimed a hero. The Lafitte brothers and their men were pardoned by order of President Madison on February 6, 1815.

So take a chance and venture a ways down Bourbon Street away from the more touristy places. The bar is flush with the street and its open doors are inviting. Sitting on the sidewalk in front of Lafitte's

Blacksmith Bar with a drink in hand is one of the greatest people-watching experiences to be had. There is no cover charge for entry into the bar . . . nor any set closing time for departing the bar. So chill! Sit in the front bar around antique wooden tables where a central fireplace warms the damp stone walls, or move toward the back where local musicians heat up the room by tickling the ivories of an old grand piano and belting out requests from guests who bravely (liquor induced, no doubt) sing along. Todd Thompson was making his way into the bar when I asked him what was so special about Lafitte's. "It's a part of history and the oldest bar in the US. That's what makes it cool," replied Thompson. The celebrity wall is worth checking out too.

Lafitte's atmosphere is unmatched—the tavern has no interior electrical lighting and only flickering candles illuminate the dark-wooded interior, giving the bar a dark, mysterious ambience. Some say you can't see your hand in front of your face or the faces of your drinking companions, and maybe that's an added plus to the dim lighting. If the weather is good, you can have a drink in the courtyard out back. Lafitte's famous Hurricanes are $8, and are reputed to be the best, and strongest, in town. They come in souvenir plastic cups, so if you have to leave early, you can take one to go. Bloody Marys, garnished with pickled green beans, are said to be "the best on earth!" Beers are about $4, mixed drinks start at $5. Locally brewed Abita beer is on tap. Of course, you have to try the bar's signature Voodoo Daiquiri, a grape-flavored slushy drink made with bourbon and 190-proof Everclear. Reputed to have serious magical powers, this is a favorite of tourists and locals alike. Not into purple drinks? One customer said that he had the strongest Maker's and Coke here that he had ever been served in a bar. There is waiter service to the tables and if you are taking a carriage ride through the Quarter, have your horse . . . or mule stop outside Lafitte's for curbside drink service.

The old building looks as if it could collapse at any moment, but it's a great place to enjoy a drink . . . or two, or more and maybe look around for evidence of hidden treasure. Some say Lafitte's booty is still secreted within the walls of the blacksmith shop bar. In 1970 Lafitte's Blacksmith Shop was certified as a National Historic Landmark and, perhaps more importantly, is listed as one of *Esquire's* "Best Bars in America."

LA PHARMACIE FRANÇAISE

514 CHARTRES ST. • NEW ORLEANS, LA 70130

(504) 565-8028 • PHARMACYMUSEUM.ORG

Very Eerie, Indeed!

Where would we be without modern medicine? Visit La Pharmacie Française, one of the nation's largest and most diverse collections of pharmaceutical items, and see exhibits of old patent medicines, ancient pharmaceutical equipment and books, and blood-sucking leeches.

There is also a newly renovated courtyard and herb garden, but that's getting ahead of ourselves. When you cross the threshold of La Pharmacie Française you enter another time and place, the world of early pharmaceutical arts and Louis Joseph Dufilho Jr. (sometimes spelled Duffalo).

Dufilho's family immigrated to New Orleans in 1803. His father, Jean, and brother, Louis, were already "pharmaciens" licensed in France, and when young Louis Joseph came of age, he was sent to the School of Pharmacy in Paris. While he was in France, Louisiana achieved statehood and new laws were set in place for pharmacists. Dufilho was required to pass a 3-hour Louisiana pharmacy license exam. On May 11, 1816, Dufilho did so and became the first pharmacist to earn a US-issued license to practice.

After practicing for a few years, Dufilho bought two lots at 514/516 Chartres St. and opened his apothecary in 1823. He operated his pharmacy until 1855 when, after more than 30 years of practice, he moved back to France where he died the next year. His apothecary was then occupied by Dr. James Dupas, a pharmacist and physician surrounded by tales of strange occurrences: People were seen to enter the apothecary, but never leave. It seems Dr. Dupas was

engaged in experimental pharmacology and carried out bizarre experiments until his death in 1867. He is said to have gone mad.

Today you can see the beautifully carved rosewood cabinets that hid Dupas's scissors-like urethral dilators, blood-letting knives, primitive drills for boring into skulls, and eye scalpels as well as narcotics, herbal tonics, magical Oriental oils, lithium, cocaine, and heroin. His healing concoctions were made from poisons and ingredients used in the practice of voodoo.

In the years following Dupas's death the building saw many owners, but none held onto the property for very long. In 1915 a devastating hurricane ravaged the area and the once vibrant pharmacy stood vacant and neglected for more than 20 years. In 1937 then-mayor Robert Maestri bought the building and donated it to the city. Maestri established the Historical Pharmacy Commission of the City of New Orleans, which began plans for turning the building into a museum. After extensive repair and renovation the museum was officially dedicated on October 16, 1950 and was operated by the city commission until 1987 when it was sold to the nonprofit preservation group, Friends of the Historical Pharmacy.

Today the New Orleans Pharmacy Museum displays the country's largest pharmaceutical collection of medical and dental artifacts of the time period in beautiful hand-carved mahogany and glass cabinets. Numerous mortars and pestles, the centuries-old emblem of pharmacy, are on display. In the front window show globes are on exhibit. Back in the day, pharmacists would fill clear globes, fancy or plain, multi-tiered or simple, with colored water to entice patrons into their shops. The globes were functional too. During plagues or epidemics, the water in the globes would be red to warn citizens of the danger of sickness lurking in their city.

The museum has two floors of exhibits. The squeaky wooden first floor is a replica of an operating apothecary, including a soda fountain (not in operation) from 1855. Here you can see displays of blood-letting equipment, microscopes, and cosmetics of the 19th century in rosewood cabinets. At the prescription counter you can learn how the pharmacist prepared and filled vintage bottles with voodoo potions, herbs, and opium and cocaine drugs used during the period. The second floor displays an examination room with hospital bed and surgical instruments, including archaic child-birthing devices, antique wheelchairs, primitive crutches, inhalers, and spectacles.

In the courtyard behind the apothecary and hidden from street traffic, you can view herbs and flowers used in the pharmacy trade years ago: Aloe was put on burns, jasmine was used to settle the stomach, foxglove was employed as a powerful heart stimulant, and Angel's Trumpet could relieve the symptoms of asthma. Culinary herbs, such as chives, tarragon, spearmint, parsley, and sweet marjoram are here too.

Dr. Dupas got away with murder, it is true, but life after death sometimes has a way of evening the score and it seems Dr. Dupas cannot rest in peace. Museum staff members say they have seen Dupas's spirit wearing a white lab coat over a brown suit on the stairway to the second floor. The ghost hunters of the International Society for Paranormal Research (ISPR) report extreme negative energy in the New Orleans Pharmacy Museum.

In New Orleans we see the best and the worst. One man left his mark on history as the first licensed pharmacist in the country; the other engaged in bizarre human experimentation for which he is sentenced to roam La Pharmacie Française forever. Check it out yourself! Entrance fees are $5 for adults, $4 for seniors and students, and children under 6 are admitted free. La Pharmacie Française is open Tuesday–Saturday, 10 a.m. to 4 p.m.; guided tours are Tuesday–Friday at 1 p.m.

LE PETIT THÉÂTRE
DU VIEUX CARRÉ

616 ST. PETER ST. • NEW ORLEANS, LA 70116

(504) 522-2081 • LEPETITTHEATRE.COM

A Very Illustrious Community Playhouse

*L*e Petit Théâtre du Vieux Carré can be translated as The Little French Quarter Theater, but most locals simply refer to the city's cultural heart as Le Petit. The theater operates from a complex of intertwined restored buildings at the corner of St. Peter and Chartres Streets.

This space was designed as a townhome in the city of Nouvelle Orleans by renowned French architect Gilberto Guillemard in 1789 and built in 1794 by Jean Baptiste Orso, a wealthy New Orleanian. Before the year was out, on December 8, 1794, a major fire ravaged the city, destroying 212 buildings, including the Orso house. Since Spain now controlled New Orleans as a result of the 1763 Treaty of Paris, the city was forced to conform to new building codes. These building requirements would transform an old French town into a modern Spanish city. Spanish baked tiles and quarried slate replaced cypress-shingled roofs, and Spanish inner courtyards and decorative iron work became popular motifs. The house was rebuilt and in 1797 it served as the residence of the last Spanish governor of Louisiana, Don Manuel Gayoso de Lemos, who was famous for his edict declaring Catholicism as the official faith of the colony. The building sits on the edge of Jackson Square near the St. Louis Cathedral and the Cabildo, the seat of government for the Louisiana province while it was being batted back and forth between France and Spain and ultimately the US. The structure saw its share of the comings and going of the rich and poor, the politically powerful, and the religiously motivated.

Ravaged by civil war occupation, deadly yellow fever epidemics, and the disintegration of inner cities, the property eventually fell into disrepair.

In 1922, supported by a growing base of local theater-lovers, the Drama League of America needed a larger performance area than the drawing rooms of patrons, and so the group, under the guidance of Mrs. James Oscar Nixon, purchased the land on St. Peter Street. Three dilapidated structures were removed and famed architect Richard Koch designed a new theater in the old Spanish Colonial style. The corner building, the one dating back to 1797, though in bad shape, was left intact. This historic structure persevered into the 20th century and in 1963 was renovated to complete the theater's collection of buildings, reception rooms, offices, and dressing rooms, as well as the Children's Corner Theatre. In 2012 the theater underwent a major multimillion-dollar renovation and is today a professionally equipped venue. Part of the property was sold to the Brennan family of restaurateurs, providing them a space for Tableau at Le Petit Théâtre, a contemporary Louisiana restaurant that offers a unique dining experience for theatergoers.

Le Petit is one of the oldest continuously operating community theaters in the US. The playhouse is equipped with professional lighting, state-of-the-art sound equipment, and well-furnished dressing rooms. The main theater has a seating capacity of 450. All the performers at Le Petit are volunteers, according to its community theater charter rules, but many guest artists and professional performers have worked here as well. Ellen DeGeneres, comedian and TV talk show host, and New Orleans native, referred to her connection to Le Petit in a website post in 2009. Other stars connected to Le Petit are Harry Connick Jr. and Wynton Marsalis.

Today Le Petit is a premier venue for performance and cultural events from lavish Broadway performances, such as its recent offering of the rock opera *Jesus Christ Superstar*, to more intimate productions such as *Dinner with Friends*. Le Petit also hosts several literary festivals every year. One of the longest running and most notable is the Tennessee Williams Festival held annually in late March to celebrate the playwright's birthday. You can enjoy topical and timely literary, and not so literary, panel discussions, performances of his plays, and even a "Stella-shouting" contest on one of the French Quarter balconies. Take a look at upcoming events at Le Petit as you plan your trip to the Big Easy. I have been here many times for various types of productions and can say that there is not a bad seat in this small performance space. The theater boasts ivied balconies with antique wrought-iron railings and a lush inner courtyard with a bubbling fountain that insulates theatergoers from the raucous behavior outside on the French Quarter streets. You won't want to miss this opportunity to be transported back in time . . . and, oh, yes, there have been reports of several "ghosts" who roam the old building. Caroline, a young actress and victim of unrequited love who threw herself off the inner balcony, has been seen walking around the second floor wearing a wedding gown, and Sigmund, a stage carpenter who died in the theater, is often accused of hiding things and playing practical jokes on the cast and crew. Enjoy the show!

LOUIS ARMSTRONG PARK

701 N. RAMPART ST. • NEW ORLEANS, LA 70116

(504) 658-3200 • NOLA.GOV/PARKS-AND-PARKWAYS/

PARKS-SQUARES/CONGO-SQUARE-LOUIS-ARMSTRONG-PARK

"What a Wonderful World"

Visually and emotionally, something magical happens when you enter Louis Armstrong Park. As you pass under the massive ornamental arch you can't help but see "trees of green and skies of blue," and, unprompted, there he is in your mind's eye, Louis "Satchmo" Armstrong, singing his distinctive refrain, and the world truly does seem "wonderful."

Located on the edge of the French Quarter, Armstrong Park not only pays homage to one of its most famous celebrated native sons, but also to the many other famous jazz musicians that have contributed to the songs, musical traditions, and cultural diversity that make up New Orleans.

The park sits on the site once designated by the leaders of the Spanish-controlled city (late 18th century) as the area where slaves would be allowed to gather on Sundays. They would use their day off to celebrate their sparse lives in bondage. Many would sing, dance, or play homemade musical instruments. Others would relax, enjoy a picnic lunch, and visit with family members. Drums, bells, and other crude musical instruments could be heard across the square and then the singing and dancing would begin. This area became known as Congo Square, a name that is still used in reference to this section of the park, now registered as a National Landmark. This gathering place and the 31 acres of park now enclosed in the park have such a rich African history. It borders on the Tremé district, which was one of the first neighborhoods created by and for African Americans.

After the Civil War, white city leaders tried to suppress the gatherings of freed slaves in the park and officially renamed Congo Square as "Beauregard Square" after the former Confederate general P. G. T. Beauregard. Despite the controlling efforts of the powerful elite, the area continued to be used for social meetings and joyous occasions. No longer relegated to just Sunday, the park became an area much in demand for fairs and fests. And despite the formal name change, residents continued to refer to the area as Congo Square. The popularity of Congo Square was in evidence when plans were formulated for what was to become a huge annual event, the New Orleans Jazz and Heritage Festival. The first two festivals (1970 and 1971) were held here in Congo Square. At the time, the Jazz Festival cost $3 for admission and minimally advertised its one gospel tent and four open stages, most of which did not even have microphones. Visiting musicians were housed in friends' homes nearby. Pete Fountain and the Clyde Kerr orchestras kicked off the festivities by playing on a Wednesday night steamboat ride, and Mahalia Jackson, who just "heard" about the event, showed up to sing.

Organizers of the first festival had no idea what to expect in terms of attendance, but they hoped that the appearances of The

Preservation Hall Band, Duke Ellington, Pete Fountain, Al Hirt, Clifton Chenier, Fats Domino, The Meters, and Snooks Eaglin would encourage people to come out the following year.

This first lineup had an audience of only 350 people, but that number was to skyrocket in the future. After 2 years, the Jazz Fest crowds had outgrown the original space and required a larger venue. It moved from Armstrong Park to the nearby New Orleans Fair Grounds racetrack. In 2001, an estimated 650,000 people attended the 7-day celebration, and while attendance numbers suffered after the impact of Hurricane Katrina, attendance had climbed to above the 450,000 mark in 2014. The name Congo Square was finally formalized by the New Orleans City Council in 2011, and in a salute to the origins of the festival there still is a "Congo Square Stage" at Jazz Fest.

There's a lot to experience within the park on your visit. This area is also the home to the Mahalia Jackson Theater of the Performing Arts, completely renovated after Hurricane Katrina and a vital, vibrant gathering place for many cultural events in the city.

Today Armstrong Park hosts annual Martin Luther King Jr. Day celebrations, weddings, and festivals. The park is often the site of movie premieres for films made in New Orleans, operas, and Broadway productions such as *Lion King*, *Wicked*, and *Jersey Boys*. Its graceful crystal chandeliers decorate the venue, which provides seating for 2,100 people. Armstrong Park's performance center is set amid quiet lagoons and weeping willow trees, and intermission during events is a time for patrons to stroll around and take in the beauty of the area.

The park is open year-round, and is just a short walk across Rampart Street, the dividing line separating the Tremé neighborhood from the French Quarter. When planning your visit, you also might want to drop in on one of the residents of St. Louis Cemetery No. 1. Created in 1789, the cemetery is located at Basin and St. Louis Streets and is one of New Orleans's most famous "cities of the dead." St. Louis Cemetery No. 1 was immortalized in the film *Easy Rider* and is the final resting place of civil rights activist Homer Plessy and New Orleans's most famous voodoo queen, Marie Laveau.

If you walk farther up from Armstrong Park to the corner of Governor Nicholls Street and St. Claude Avenue, you will find the impressive St. Augustine Church, which was built in 1842 by free people of color. It is the oldest African-American Catholic Church in the country.

Plan a lazy afternoon of walking, eating, sunning, and experiencing Louis Armstrong Park and all the neighborhood has to offer. History literally jumps out at you at every turn of the corner and helps you realize that New Orleans is so much more than Bourbon Street and beignets.

LOUISIANA'S CIVIL WAR MUSEUM

929 CAMP ST. • NEW ORLEANS, LA 70130

(504) 523-4522 • CONFEDERATEMUSEUM.COM

Oldest Museum in the State of Louisiana

*L*ouisiana's Civil War Museum sits in the shadow of its giant counterpart, the much-celebrated and sprawling National World War II Museum that opened in New Orleans on June 6, 2000, as the National D-day Museum. But as the oldest continuously operating museum in the state, the Civil War Museum can rightfully claim its place in the sun. And adding to its splendor, it is housed in one of the most architecturally beautiful buildings in the city, in stark contrast to the World War II Museum's modern structure just across the street.

Originally called the Confederate Memorial Hall, the Civil War Museum had its beginning some 30 years after the American Civil War when a group of men banded together to discuss the possibility of a museum to house donated Confederate relics and act as a repository of war records. Led by a leading local philanthropist, Frank Howard, a 25-member Board of Governors comprising members from local Confederate veterans associations was established with the objective to preserve, honor, and remember the lives and events of the Civil War. They organized the Louisiana Historical Association, and the Confederate Memorial Hall opened its doors on January 8, 1891. The museum soon expanded to include veterans associations beyond Louisiana, reaching out to member groups such as the Army of Tennessee, the Army of Northern Virginia, the Washington Artillery, and the Association of Confederate States Cavalry. To support the expansion, Howard entirely funded the construction of an annex called Memorial Hall and turned it over to the Louisiana Historical Society in 1891.

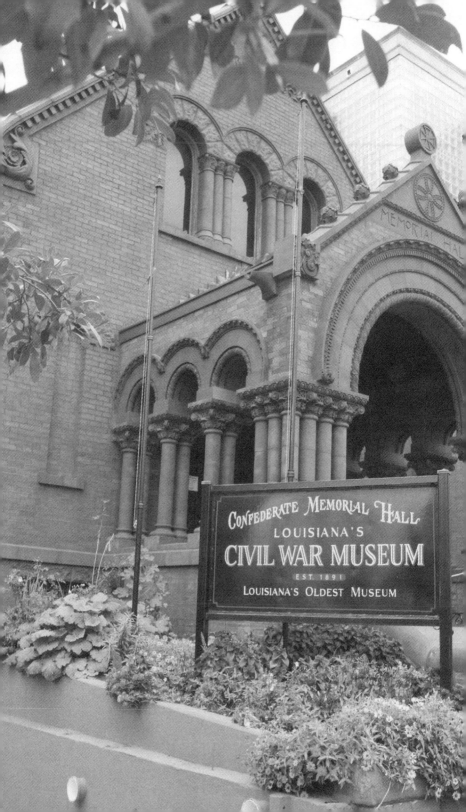

On your visit to the museum, be sure to admire the openness of the interior design. The New Orleans *Daily Picayune* (now the *Times Picayune*) reported: "Brown stone steps head gently upward to the entrance (where) a massive door constructed of southern cypress, (is) finished in oil and suspended with antique hinges. Within is a wonderland. The hall is open and continuous . . . Above are beams giving an impression of strength and fixity, and above them a lengthwise ridge of glass windows on both sides, affording a plentiful flow of light."

As much as you might appreciate both the design and architecture of the building, it is the contents, collected over nearly 120 years, that are amazing. You can see more than 140 regimental flags, the most famous of which is the flag that adorned the coffin of Confederate president Jefferson Davis. Memorial Hall was the place where the city bid farewell to Jefferson Davis, who died in 1889. There are a lot of Confederate uniforms on display. The variety of styles and colors is very interesting. While officers' uniforms appear to have much the same tailoring with ornate epaulets and sashes, enlisted men's uniforms were very plain, but varying in both fabric and color. It's obvious that the Confederate army did not have the resources to outfit their regiments.

Weaponry is also on display. You are welcomed to the museum by a large Columbiad, a Civil War cannon that is mounted on the front terrace. You can view a rare display of an early hand-grenade, and period rifles, cannon, and muskets show the progression of firearms. Swords, in a variety of ornate styles, were used to represent status and prestige in combat and visitors can view a number of these.

Most prominent among the exhibits are the personal items donated over the years by families and friends of former Confederate soldiers. You can get a glimpse of a set of field eating utensils inscribed "For a Good Boy," and a sewing kit called a "housewife" made to resemble a Confederate flag. One prized museum piece is a chess set carved of wood by a prisoner confined to a prisoner of war camp in the North. There are also personal items that once belonged to Generals Robert E. Lee and P. G. T. Beauregard.

Aside from the museum pieces, there are continuous exhibits depicting various battles and special events in an effort to bring greater understanding of the struggles, hardships, and tactical

✎*Vintage Spot*

THE NATIONAL WORLD WAR II MUSEUM: EST. 2000

Journalist Tom Brokaw coined the phrase "The Greatest Generation" when describing those Americans who grew up during the Great Depression and then went on to fight and help support by their labors the freedoms of oppressed people around the world.

The National World War II Museum tells the story of their experiences in gripping detail, from D-day at Normandy to the battles in the Pacific and the Solomon Islands, and so much more. But the stories here are not just about the servicemen and women who gave their lives or were fortunate enough to survive to tell their stories. The exhibits are, as founder, historian, and author Stephen Ambrose says, "the story of the American experience in *the war that changed the world*—why it was fought, how it was won, and what it means today—so that all generations will understand the price of freedom and be inspired by what they learn."

The displays are not just for history buffs or high school teachers. They are for all people who treasure liberty. A visit to the World War II Museum is not only a learning experience; it is the chance to understand.

**945 Magazine St.; (504) 528-1944;
nationalww2museum.org**

planning of the war. One recent exhibit featured the Red River Campaign, a series of battles in 1864 that were fought both on land and on the waterways of north and central Louisiana.

Louisiana's Civil War Museum is open Tuesday through Saturday from 10 a.m. to 4 p.m. Just outside the museum at Lee Circle you can also see the 16-foot statue of General Robert E. Lee atop a 60-foot white marble pedestal. The monument was erected in 1884. Be sure to note that Lee faces due north, ever keeping the enemy in sight.

MOTHER-IN-LAW LOUNGE

1500 N. CLAIBORNE AVE. • NEW ORLEANS, LA 70116

(504) 947-1078 • K-DOE.COM

Only in Funky and Fantastic New Orleans!

*A*re you ready for some real New Orleans–style entertainment? The Mother-in-Law Lounge, at the edge of New Orleans's historic Tremé neighborhood, is truly a unique experience. You will have to drive or take a taxi to this Seventh Ward ultra-funky establishment on the corner of N. Claiborne and Columbus Street. You might even get to hear some live music from the Tremé Brass Band or perhaps enjoy some "good eatin'" of fried chicken, red beans and rice, and biscuits. There's really no agenda here, other than being happy, but the drinks are reasonably priced and there's dancing. I don't even know how to begin to tell you the history of the flamboyant musician who started the lounge and what happened to him. But I will try.

The Mother-in-Law Lounge is dedicated to its founder Ernie K-Doe, local R&B singer and character extraordinaire. K-Doe, born in 1936 as Ernest Kador Jr., started out singing in church and with various spiritual groups, such as the Golden Choir Jubilees of New Orleans and the Divine Travelers. At the age of 15, he was "discovered" while performing at an amateur talent show by the manager of the legendary Flamingos. K-Doe always moved "with the spirit" and worked to perfect his signature dancing with microphone in hand, falling down, and even rolling off the stage. He enjoyed stints at the Apollo Theater, the Howard Theater, the Uptown Theater, the Regal Theater, and Carnegie Hall. Many of you might remember his biggest hit song, "Mother-in-Law (1961)," with lyrics: "Satan should be her name. To me they're bout the same. She thinks her advice is the constitution. But if she would leave, that would be the solution. And don't come back

no more, Mother-in-law." Because of its offensive lyrics, the song was banned from Dick Clark's influential *American Bandstand* television show. Of course this only added to the song's popularity. "Mother-in-Law" made it to No. 1 on both the Billboard pop and R&B charts.

Hard times were to follow for the young man. Years later, back on his home turf in New Orleans, K-Doe was trying to stage a comeback. He opened the Ernie K-Doe Mother-in-Law Lounge in 1994 to provide a performance venue for himself and other local living legends. He performed in a pink tuxedo, gold crown, and cape and declared himself "Emperor of the Universe." One of the eccentric showman's most memorable performances was at the Aquarium of the Americas in the French Quarter. Dressed in a green-plumed cape, he gyrated wildly in front of the shark tank and sang seven continuous rounds of "Mother-in-Law." K-Doe was inducted into the Louisiana and New Orleans music halls of fame and received the prestigious Rhythm & Blues Foundation Pioneer award in 1997 at Radio City Music Hall, where he brought down the house with his performance of "Mother-in-Law." In 1999, Ernie K-Doe was the first person to be honored with the Big Easy Entertainment Heritage Award.

Shortly before his death in 2001, he received a lifetime achievement award from Louisiana governor Mike Foster. K-Doe had performed in the Crescent City for over 50 years and his jazz funeral and second-line procession was one of New Orleans's all-time greatest celebrations. Afterward, his wife Antoinette sat a life-size mannequin of K-Doe in his regular chair at the lounge and moved him around to sit in on conversations or face the stage to watch performers. After Hurricane Katrina's waters receded, the lounge reopened with help from local musicians, the national Hands-on Network, and superstar recording artist and producer Usher. Antoinette led a mock campaign for K-Doe's election for mayor of the hurricane-ravaged city, disregarding the fact that K-Doe had been dead for 5 years. Antoinette said, "He's the only one qualified."

Royalty needs a palace. Today you can party in the Emperor of the Universe's flamboyant, awe-inspiring, two-story memorial. Local artist Daniel Fuselier, known for his Mardi Gras float designs, has been described as the Michelangelo of the Mother-in-Law Lounge. Fuselier took more than 7 years to paint the outdoor K-Doe murals that cover the entire building as a labor of love, not taking a penny for his efforts. On one of the blue cracked-stuccoed façades of the building you can see Clarence "Frogman" Henry and Al "Carnival Time" Johnson. Another wall features K-Doe and Antoinette with hearts entwined. True to her dramatic flair, Antoinette suffered a fatal heart attack on Mardi Gras morning in 2009; she died behind the counter at the Mother-in-Law Lounge.

Today the lounge is a shrine to the immortal legend of K-Doe. The walls are adorned with photographs of family and friends. The life-size figure of K-Doe is no longer at the lounge, and that has regulars wondering, "Where did K-Doe go?" Relax, have a drink, and play the jukebox, which has a fantastic selection of classic New Orleans R&B artists' songs and many K-Doe hits. Don't be surprised if you find yourself rubbing elbows with some of the greats of the Crescent City when you visit the Mother-in-Law Lounge. They like to stop in to remember old times and kick back with new owner Kermit Ruffins, local jazz trumpeter, singer, and composer. If you get the chance, look for a staging of *Burn K-Doe Burn* while you are in New Orleans. The irreverent show is a combination of history and legend . . . and not to be missed! Bands perform at the Mother-in-Law Lounge on Monday, Wednesday, and Friday. Ruffins says that he is trying to bring in musicians on Saturday and Sunday as well. The lounge reopened on Martin Luther King Day, 2014. Check the website for the entertainment schedule (still in flux) and for the hours (still in flux) the lounge is open.

MOTHER'S

401 POYDRAS ST. • NEW ORLEANS, LA 70130

(504) 523-9656 • MOTHERSRESTAURANT.NET

A Sandwich Just Like Mother Makes

*I*f you have never considered standing in line for a sandwich in your life, you might want to think about it during your next visit to New Orleans!

Mother's Restaurant, offering a menu as culturally rich and diverse as its daily clientele, has been cooking up delectable and mouthwatering food since before World War II. But while the landscape around the rather unimposing storefront has dramatically transformed over the past 70+ years and ownership has changed hands three times, the eating experience inside has become world-famous.

Founders Simon and Mary (Mother) Landry opened the restaurant in 1938, mainly serving po'boys, the New Orleans version of subs or hero sandwiches. However, the difference was that these "sandwiches," whether hot or cold, were served on French bread and literally stuffed with meats, cheeses, and a variety of special spices and gravy.

According to the website, while their original customers were mainly longshoremen, laborers, newspapermen, and local attorneys, the ensuing world war and the fact that five of the seven Landry children signed up for the Marine Corps established the eatery as the unofficial headquarters for "the few and the proud" . . . Marine Corps service personnel who shared a common bond and camaraderie with the family. After all, daughter Francis Landry was the first woman in Louisiana to be accepted into this proud and heroic branch of the military.

After the war, sons Jacques and Eddie took over the running of the business, continuing to expand the menu and the fine reputation their parents had established. In 1986 they sold the beloved food hangout to two young enterprising brothers, Jerry and John Amato, who added delectable dishes such as Jambalaya and Shrimp Creole and "customized" po'boys to include the Ferdi, Ralph, and Debris . . . named after special customers who frequented the renowned destination restaurant.

Over the years, Jerry, who assumed the head chef role, ensured allegiance to the original flavoring of the truly New Orleans style of cooking, but also added so much more to attract hungry customers from around the world. It is reported that in a typical week, Mother's cooks up 800–1,000 pounds of shrimp, 60–70 gallons of oysters, and 200 pounds each of catfish and crawfish!

The seating area has expanded over the years, but don't expect a new, modern addition, because the owners kept the look and feel of the original Mother's. You can look around the interior and see the long history of the restaurant. As you await your order, you can often find yourself in the middle of a food drama as orders are shouted out over the heads of customers, plates clank and clatter nearby, and bustling waiters hurriedly sidestep the take-out line to get your food to you. Like so many businesses in New Orleans, Mother's was not spared the wrath of Hurricane Katrina, and while the damage was minimal, it took more than a month of intensive clean-up and preparation before the restaurant could reopen its doors.

During the Katrina clean-up, there were nine FEMA trailers in the Mother's parking lot to house the restaurant staff. Many of these loyal employees had lost everything to the storm, but not their jobs nor their love for their Mother's family. Vice Admiral Thad Allen, head of the disaster relief effort in New Orleans, was the first customer through the doors when Mother's reopened.

You cannot make a reservation at Mother's, but if you want to minimize your time in the food line outside the restaurant, try getting up a little earlier in the morning and head to Poydras Street for breakfast. You will find the doors open and many other customers who had the same idea, but you won't be disappointed with the food choices and the ample portions that await you, and relax . . . so what if you have to wait a while for perfection!

If breakfast isn't your thing, you can enjoy lunch or dinner, with food combinations that you have never experienced before. And whatever you do, leave room for some authentic New Orleans bread pudding.

Aside from the enjoyment of eating in a place that is recognized as a "must do, must see, must eat" destination, it's comforting that Mother's has survived in its original form, regardless of financial hardships, dramatic changes, and the constant movement toward the "bigger is better" concept of so many other business.

So, set aside an hour or so on your next (or first) visit to the Big Easy, and put Mother's restaurant at the top of your bucket list. It's a great place for an after-game meal and, whether your team won or lost, you will remember your experience at Mother's for years to come. If you feel an obligation to bring the kids a present, check out the gift shop!

MUSÉE CONTI WAX MUSEUM

917 RUE CONTI • NEW ORLEANS, LA 70112

(504) 525-2605 • NEWORLEANSWAXMUSEUM.COM

What's Napoleon Doing in a Bathtub in New Orleans?

The French Quarter is full of inviting bars, souvenir shops, and great eating places. But if you want to learn about the history of New Orleans in a unique and fun way, head on down to the Musée Conti on Conti Street between Dauphine and Burgundy Streets and 1½ blocks from Bourbon Street. Billed as "The Historical Wax Museum of New Orleans," the exhibits recreate the fascinating world of French Creoles as the story of New Orleans unfolds before your eyes. Unbelievable stories are woven into the city's history, starting with the European discovery of the area over 300 years ago. You will meet local legends such as Iberville and Bienville contemplating the swampy area with the Choctaw Indians, John Law and the duc d'Orleans planning the city of New Orleans, and Napoleon selling Louisiana to the US from a bathtub. The tour features other New Orleans legends such as Mardi Gras Zulu King Weatherspoon and Louis Armstrong.

The wax museum is housed in an old two-story slate-roofed Creole town house built in 1890. The building is a surviving example of turn of the century French Quarter architecture featuring cypress windows, interior brick walls, and exposed wooden beams. The original heartwood pine floors are still intact. The museum is on the bottom floor and upstairs, behind the beautiful, floor-to-ceiling leaded glass windows, is the Legend Room where locals gather to celebrate weddings, corporate events, and private parties.

You and the family will love the wax museum! In fact, the museum was the first family attraction in the French Quarter, opened in 1964

by the Lazarus and Weil families. Isadore Lazarus and Ben Weil had taken a trip to Madame Tussaud's in London and decided New Orleans needed a similar museum to depict its notable, and sometimes notorious, history. Lazarus and Weil put up the required $250,000 funding and after 3 years of planning and preparation, the museum finally opened. John Churchill Chase, historical researcher and advisor, insisted that all of the figures and costumes match the actual height and size proportions of the historic figures. People are often astonished at the diminutive stature of some of the wax figurines, but statistics show the human race has been steadily getting taller, especially over the last hundred years. The early figures were made mostly in Paris using beeswax mixed with an ingredient that caused the wax to stiffen and become slightly transparent. Flesh-toned coloring was then added beneath the waxy layer to make the statue appear more lifelike. The glass eyes of figures are made in Germany, a country long known for its expertise in optical glass. All full-size figures have real human hair imported from Italy and each strand is inserted separately using a special needle in a very labor-intensive process. To provide further realism, the beards of the male figures are full and complete and the shaven figures are provided with faint stubbles.

The scenes and costumes are all historically accurate as well. The original costumes for these figures, small or not, cost around $750 per outfit; that would be nearly $5,000 each today. The museum includes photos of the wax figures being made.

The museum consists of several sections. Thirty-one scenes of 147 life-size figures depict 300 years of Louisiana history, chronologically, from 1699 through 1910. There are some additional wax models of famous figures from the later 1900s. A popular miniature scene features a Mardi Gras parade, circa 1900, marching down the 400 block of Royal Street. Miniature wax figures include mule-drawn floats with riders and spectators on the street leaning out of buildings. Balloons, made from hollowed-out pigeon eggs, decorate the festive scene.

The "Haunted Dungeon" section of wax figures features famous characters from horror films and literature. In the chamber of horrors you can see depictions of "The Body Snatchers," a story by Robert Louis Stevenson, and "The Pit and the Pendulum" by Edgar Allan Poe. You can also view characters such as Bram Stoker's Dracula, Mary Shelley's monster from *Frankenstein*, as well as the Hunchback of Notre Dame and the Phantom of the Opera.

Wax figures have been around since the days of Babylon. Alexander the Great had his own wax sculptor and the Romans practiced the art of wax sculpting. No medieval fair was complete without its wax figures. The museum's website says, "We believe that the Musée Conti Wax Museum is a worthy successor to this long and firmly rooted tradition." This treasure trove of legend and scandal is yours for the admission price of $8 for adults, $7.25 for seniors, and $7 for children ages 4 to 17. The Musée Conti Wax Museum is open Monday, Friday, and Saturday from 10 a.m. to 4 p.m.; it is closed on major holidays. Program guides are available in French, Italian, Spanish, German, and Japanese.

So, if you want to learn how the game of craps came to the US or how the Bowie knife got its name, saunter on down to the Musée Conti Wax Museum. Don't be afraid to visit Madam LaLaurie and view evidence of her heinous crimes. It's a story from the city's past that is well documented, but not talked about much. And don't panic if you catch a glimpse of the Creature from the Black Lagoon. He lives here too!

NEW CANAL LIGHTHOUSE
MUSEUM & EDUCATION CENTER

8001 LAKESHORE DR. • NEW ORLEANS, LA 70124

(504) 836-2215 • SAVEOURLAKE.ORG

The Lakefront View Is Spectacular!

It's time to leave the French Quarter for a while and head out to Lake Pontchartrain for some fun and recreation. Pack a lunch, bring your bicycle, or plan a stroll along the lakefront seawall. Locals make good use of this area for family reunions, ball games, quiet drives, dining, fishing, summer parties, sailing, and much more.

A good starting point for exploring the area is the New Canal Lighthouse. Although the building was severely damaged by Hurricanes Katrina and Rita in 2005, the extensive reconstruction of the lighthouse is now complete and its beacon, re-lit ceremoniously in September 2012, once again shines nightly for all to see.

You can stroll through the lighthouse museum and education center and find fascinating information about the ecology of the Lake Pontchartrain Basin and its role in the development of New Orleans. You can also learn about the history of the lighthouse and see the Fresnel lens believed to have been in the lighthouse since the early 1900s.

Future plans include a dock, but that still needs funding. If you want to be a part of this 175-year-old lighthouse's history and leave your mark on New Orleans while helping to fund further reconstruction efforts, you can purchase a personalized brick for yourself or as a gift. For $200 you can put three lines of text (up to 18 characters per line) on a brick that will be installed at the museum site. You will receive a commemorative certificate authenticating your support and notification when your brick is installed and a map indicating where you can find your brick on the site.

Way back in 1839, the original lighthouse was commissioned by an act of Congress that authorized $25,000 for a structure with beacons to be constructed on the New Basin Canal at the entrance to the Lake Pontchartrain harbor. The lighthouse was basically a cypress tower on pilings set a thousand feet offshore with a lantern on top. On March 10, 1863, the lighthouse beacon was extinguished by order of General Sherman, commander of the defenses in New Orleans during the Civil War.

The lighthouse survived the war and by 1869 was once again casting its beam across the harbor. But the equipment was antiquated. In 1890 the lighthouse was sold at public auction for scrap and a new structure, consisting of a square, two-story white frame building with a slate roof, was constructed on iron pilings. Now the new lantern could illuminate 270 degrees of the horizon from a point 49 feet above sea level. This is the lighthouse building-style you will see today. In 1915, a 12-foot storm surge and 130 mph winds from a devastating Category 4 hurricane (hurricanes did not have names yet) destroyed much of the lighthouse bulkhead. But repairs and updates were made. A Category 3 hurricane in 1926 again damaged the structure and this time the lighthouse was set onto concrete piers. After Hurricanes Katrina and Rita once again destroyed the lighthouse, a precise replica of the New Canal Lighthouse was built incorporating some of the original wood from the 1890 lighthouse.

On December 30, 1985, the New Canal Lighthouse was placed on the National Register of Historic Places. The United States Coast Guard (USCG) occupied and operated the lighthouse from the 1960s until 2001, but before the USCG there were lighthouse keepers. Local women stand out in lighthouse history. Elizabeth Beattie was appointed lighthouse keeper in 1847 after her husband, the station's first keeper, died. Other notable figures include Jane O'Driscol, Mary Campbell, and Caroline Riddle, who was commended for her heroic efforts to keep the light lit during a raging hurricane. Maggie Norvell took over from Riddle in 1924 and is credited with saving the lives of 200 people by rowing them to shore after a fire broke out on an excursion boat.

You can visit Louisiana's only working lighthouse and enjoy its great museum and education center. A spacious balcony allows one of the most beautiful panoramic views of the New Orleans south shore lakefront you can get. Be sure to note the new red roof and cupola, which were added in 2012. The cupola of the lighthouse is not open to the public, but the light within it shines nightly to aid the navigation of private boats on the lake.

The museum is on the first floor of the rebuilt lighthouse, which now sits 19 feet above the level of Lake Pontchartrain to protect it from future storm surges. The museum can be accessed by stairs or elevator "lift" for visitors with special needs. Display areas in the museum depict the history of the structure of the lighthouse and lifesaving station and the city's continued efforts to protect the ecology of the lake. You can take a lighthouse tour led by trained docents and learn all about the animal habitats of Lake Pontchartrain.

There are numerous events associated with the lighthouse, including the Back to the Beach Festival, Beach Sweep, Fishing Rodeo, Golf Classic, the Northshore "Let's Make Waves" Party, and various arts and crafts fairs. Check the website before heading out to the lakefront.

The Lighthouse has a fountain plaza, breezeway, promenade, and deck outside and a great little gift shop inside. You will really enjoy this side trip!

The museum is open Monday through Saturday. Docent-led tours are available 10 a.m. to 4 p.m. Admission is $7.50 for adults, $5.50 for seniors, students and military, $3.00 for children ages 6–12 and children under 6 get in free. The lighthouse is about a 20-minute drive from the French Quarter by car or taxi. There is ample parking all along the shoreline. Gray Line Tours offers tours Monday through Saturday that include a guided tour of the New Canal Lighthouse. Contact Gray Line Tours at (504) 569-1401 or (800) 233-2628.

NEW ORLEANS HISTORIC VOODOO MUSEUM

724 DUMAINE ST. • NEW ORLEANS, LA 70116 • (504) 680-0128
WWW.ARTCOM.COM/MUSEUMS/VS/MR/70116-31.HTM

Not for the Faint of Heart or Those Who Get Weirded Out Easily!

Voodoo rituals, brought to New Orleans in the 1700s, are still part of the city's culture today. Just ask any little girl who's been bullied why she's sticking pins in her voodoo doll! Voodoo first came to the city from West Africa, brought by the Fon, a people of what is today the Republic of Benin, on the first slave ship arriving in Louisiana from the Slave Coast. They brought their religious practices with them to the New World. Their word for spirits was *Vodoun* and the religious practice was based in the belief that spirits interact in the daily affairs of men and women. Some slaves from Benin were also deposited on the Caribbean islands, and when Haitian refugees fled the 1791 revolution, they also brought a form of voodoo with them to New Orleans.

Voodoo was originally an underground religious practice that included voodoo queens, gris-gris spells, occult rituals, charms and amulets, dancing, singing, and celebration of the snake deity. In New Orleans, certain aspects of voodoo adapted and morphed and gradually found their way into mainstream beliefs and practices. Today, though most New Orleanians would deny that it is still practiced, some voodoo practices are still ingrained in the culture.

You'll see lots of evidence of voodoo throughout the city, especially in the French Quarter and surrounding areas that were populated early in the city's history. Love potions for sale, herbs grown for use in religious rites and rituals, and the New Orleans Voodoo team of the Arena Football League perpetuate the voodoo legacy.

To learn more about New Orleans voodoo, you can visit the Historic Voodoo Museum, which preserves this unique part of New Orleans history. This small museum offers visitors an inside look at the legends and traditions of voodoo and hoodoo (a mixture of folklore and Christian spirituality), and the cultural influence of their religious and, some would say, mysterious practices. It is jam-packed with exhibits of altars, relics, and displays. The museum is in the heart of the French Quarter and easy to find on Dumaine Street, between Royal and Bourbon Streets.

The museum was founded in 1972 by local artist Charles Massicot Gandolfo, whose ancestor was raised in New Orleans by a voodoo queen. You can read all about his family's earliest beginnings in the French colony of Saint-Domingue (Haiti) and the escape from plantation to New Orleans, by way of refugee ship, of a young mother and infant son, helped by slave and Voodoo Queen Jaquinette. Gandolfo got his name "Voodoo Charlie" from interviewer Larry King, who was down in New Orleans for the 1988 Republican National Convention in the Superdome. Interestingly, Voodoo Charlie died on Mardi Gras Day, 2001. His world-recognized portrait of voodoo queen Marie Laveau hangs in the museum. It is said that Gandolfo began the New Orleans voodoo renaissance that continues to thrive today. Currently Charles's brother Jerry Gandolfo is the Voodoo Museum's historian and researcher. He was called "Mr. Voodoo" by MSNBC and the "walking encyclopedia of New Orleans" by the local *Gambit* newspaper. The *Smithsonian Magazine* remarked on the "wooden masks, portraits, and the occasional human skull" featured in the museum's collection and noted the presence of real life voodoo priest, John T. Martin, "wearing his albino python around his neck." So don't scream if you see him and the snake taking tickets!

The museum is open daily from 10 a.m. to 6 p.m., 7 days a week. General admission is $7, students and seniors pay $5.50, high school students get in for $4.50, and elementary students will be charged $3.50. You get complimentary admission if you take the $19, 3-hour cemetery tour. If you think that may be too long of a tour, ask your guide for a "special" pecan to get rid of any potential headache.

Cameras are welcome in the museum. Questions are encouraged, so don't be afraid to ask . . . anything. Don't be afraid to step into the dark cavernous entryway. An inviting figure, identifying herself only as Carol M., welcomes whoever crosses the threshold, announcing, "We are the only voodoo museum in the country." She encourages visitors to "learn" more about voodoo. She says, "Most people are shocked that voodoo is not a negative force as portrayed on TV or in the movies." The museum offers a wide selection of voodoo items, such as Louisiana moss-stuffed voodoo dolls with blank faces so you can draw on the face of the person you want the doll to represent, 4-inch voodoo stick dolls, excellent for hiding near someone, and the all-purpose 8-inch stick doll. You can purchase a black ritual candle for meditation, a blue candle for healing, a green candle for money, a brown candle for legal situations, an orange candle for creativity, a pink candle for love, a purple candle for domination, a yellow candle for luck, or a white ritual candle for peace. All candles include appropriately colored coiled twine, feathers, and pins. The museum store also offers gris-gris bags, in various colors depending on their intended purpose, and *Voodoo in New Orleans*, a classic book on voodoo, Marie Laveau, and folklore by Robert Tallant. Feeling adventuresome? You can also purchase chicken feet, snake skins, mojo balls, voodoo kits, and a "Crossing Over" T-shirt. Looking for something more shocking? You can buy a voodoo coffin kit, Priestess Peace Oil, or a Swamp Wish doll. Most of the items are handmade in the New Orleans area and the museum's website proclaims, "Both the goods and services sold here are authentic to the traditions and practices of Voodoo." You can also get psychic readings at the museum.

OLD ABSINTHE HOUSE

240 BOURBON ST. • NEW ORLEANS, LA 70130

(504) 523-3181 • RUEBOURBON.COM/OLDABSINTHEHOUSE

When "Coffee Houses" Sold the Mean Green Liquor

On the corner of Rue Bourbon and Rue Bienville there's a sign outside a small vintage bar that reads, "Jean Lafitte's Old Absinthe House Since 1807." No trip to New Orleans would be complete without a stop here at one of the oldest structures in the French Quarter, simply called the Old Absinthe House. The flat Spanish Colonial brick building with the fanlight transoms is very much as it was when it was built; some shutters have fallen into decay and been replaced, but the building supported by exposed cypress beams still hugs the pavement and beckons to thirsty passersby.

So what should you order at the Old Absinthe House? First sit yourself down on one of the 50 barstools along the original copper-topped bar, scan the antique chandelier hanging overhead, and cast your eyes toward the authentic marble fountains with brass faucets that were once used to drip cold water over sugar cubes into glasses of absinthe. Then order one of the house specialties: the Absinthe House Frappe is refreshing and sweet—and strong—and the Absinthe Suissesse is a frothy concoction with a light minty kick.

Let your mind travel back in time to 1807 when Spaniards Pedro Front and Francisco Juncadella built the two-story entresol Creole town house. The upstairs was a residence and the ground floor served as offices for their import and trading exchange. It is said that their friend, the infamous pirate Jean Lafitte, conducted some of his business from this space and that tunnels, carved out under the building, were used to move illegal goods. Lafitte seemingly felt so

safe here that in 1814 he agreed to meet General Andrew Jackson in a private upstairs room to work on a critical plan to defeat the British at the Battle of New Orleans.

By the 1840s, the ground floor was home to a popular tavern known as "Aleix's Coffee House," run by Jacinto Aleix and his brother, nephews of the widow of Juncadella. At this time saloons were called "coffee houses" and, of course, coffee houses sold alcohol, including absinthe, the popular European anise-based, extremely addictive spirit made from the toxic wormwood herb. In 1870, the Spaniard Cayetano Ferrer left the French Opera House where he was chief mixologist and came to Aleix's Coffee House. Here he created the bar's signature drink, the Absinthe House Frappe. Absinthe was served in the Parisian manner with faucets in marble fountains dripping cold water onto lumps of sugar suspended on perforated spoons over the glass. The drink was so popular that the tavern was renamed The Absinthe Room in 1874 and 20 years later was rechristened by Ferrer's sons, now in the business, as the Old Absinthe House. The mystique of absinthe appealed to New Orleans salon society. When Edgar Degas and Oscar Wilde visited the city in the 1800s, they had no trouble finding imported French absinthes. The influence of the drink can be seen in Degas's famous painting *L'Absinthe*.

Vintage Spot

GALATOIRE'S RESTAURANT: EST. 1905

Playwright Tennessee Williams paid homage to Galatoire's, one of his favorite restaurants, in his famous play set in New Orleans, *A Streetcar Named Desire*. This culinary landmark in the heart of New Orleans is mentioned by Stella Kowalski in the play when she announces that she is "taking Blanche to Galatoire's for supper. . . ."

Founded by Jean Galatoire in 1905, the time-worn recipes and exquisite dining experience of table-white linens, real china, and silverware have changed very little over the years. Believe it or not, waiters still wear tuxedos. Galatoire's is committed to delivering captivating charm, old-world service, and southern hospitality.

The no reservations policy still holds in the main dining downstairs, but due to the reopening of an area that had been closed since World War II, you can now reserve a table upstairs. There is a Galatoire's dress code: no T-shirts or shorts at any time, and for evening dining and Sundays, a jacket is required. Don't have a jacket? No problem, the staff keeps a few jackets in various sizes to accommodate their unprepared customers.

Try the Trout Meunière (not on the menu and not always available, but be sure to ask!) and caramel custard for dessert, and don't be in a hurry . . . this eating experience and charming atmosphere are something you want to savor. You can sit, sip, eat, and enjoy the experience for as long as you like.

209 Bourbon St.; (504) 525-2021; galatoires.com

But absinthe can cause hallucinations, blindness, delirium, madness, and even death, so by the early 1900s, it was banned in the US and most of Europe. Substitutes for the wormwood herb were tried, but never caught on. The Old Absinthe House secretly operated as a speakeasy during Prohibition, but federal officers finally closed its doors in 1924. Faced with "bar burning" threats by temperance supporters, the owners moved the prized copper bar top and other furnishings to a safe warehouse. The bar reopened after Prohibition and in 2004, in a million-dollar renovation, the original bar top was returned to the Old Absinthe House. Brass figurines can be seen perching atop the fountains; the most notable figure is that of Napoleon. Past visitors to the Old Absinthe House have included P. T. Barnum, William Thackeray, Walt Whitman, Mark Twain, Aaron Burr, and Frank Sinatra. In 1934 *Time* magazine declared New Orleans the absinthe capital of the world.

A revival of drinking absinthe began in the 1990s; the European Union reauthorized the manufacture and sale of the beguiling green liquid, referred to as "la fée verte" (the Green Fairy). The US still bans the use of the wormwood plant, the original absinthe ingredient. In New Orleans, Herbsaint, a potent, locally made, anise liqueur, is used for the Absinthe Frappe. Herbsaint absinthe is said to rival the best absinthe in the world. Today, the first-floor front room of the Spanish Colonial townhome is still the Old Absinthe House with its decorative marble fountain and brass faucets. The historic building also houses the upscale Tony Moran's Restaurant, which offers Northern Italian cuisine in the rear downstairs, and on the second floor is Jean Lafitte's Bistro, which serves Cajun and Creole specialties. The bar also has a wonderful selection of fine malt scotches.

Before you leave this comfy tavern, be sure to pin your business card on the wall. There are thousands of cards decorating the walls, giving credence to the bar's motto: Everyone you have known or will know eventually ends up at the Old Absinthe House.

OLD NEW ORLEANS
RUM DISTILLERY

2815 FRENCHMEN ST. • NEW ORLEANS, LA 70122

(504) 945-9400 • OLDNEWORLEANSRUM.COM

Ho, Ho, Ho, and a Bottle of Rum!

When you think of alcohol flowing in the Big Easy, you may think of drive-through daiquiri shops or Pat O'Brien's Hurricanes toted in souvenir glasses along crowded French Quarter streets. Add these modern imbibing conveniences to the city's history of pirates and scoundrels, treasure ships and stolen booty, and the Caribbean connection to the port city. Stir in some of the area's acres and acres of sugar cane crops, and what could be more New Orleans than rum? If you want to see where some of the rum that goes into all the imaginatively named, rum-laden drinks served in bars and hotels throughout the city is produced, you can take a tour of Celebration Distillation's Old New Orleans Rum facilities.

Old New Orleans Rum was started in 1995 by James Michalopoulos, renowned New Orleans painter and sculptor. The founding group included artists, brewmasters, and engineers who wanted to produce a "more natural" variety of rum. Many rums use sugar from several pressings of sugar cane. After 2 years of distillation and engineering studies and plenty of trial and error, Old New Orleans Rum discovered a unique process that uses only sugar from the first two pressings. The company sources its molasses from local sugar cane milled at LaFourche Sugars in Thibodaux. The robust flavor comes from American oak barrels, which are charred and used only once by the finest whiskey labels. When they finally found the right combination for Old New Orleans Rum, the founders said, "Let's celebrate," and

Celebration Distillation was on its way to becoming one of the world's best rum makers, with gold medals to prove it.

The distillery is located in Gentilly, on the back streets of the Ninth Ward neighborhood, a section of New Orleans hard hit by Hurricane Katrina. It is housed in an old mid-1800s cotton warehouse that was redesigned to accommodate the distillation process. Interior brick walls and exposed wooden beams add old world ambience.

You can book a tour of Celebration Distillation on the company's website. The 45-minute tour offers a detailed look at the distillation process from step one (making the wash) to step six (blending and bottling). Old New Orleans Rum's traditional distilling uses a pot still and a column still, named for the shape of the distillation equipment. Both stills are made from aged and salvaged equipment and look as if they are as old as the building.

The cost is $10 per person and all tours start with an Old New Orleans Rum cocktail, which you can take with you on the tour. One of the cocktails you might be offered is Cajun Tea, which is made with Community tea blended with Celebration's superb Cajun Spice Rum and simple syrup.

Tours conclude with tastings of the distillery's three distinctive rums. You will have the opportunity to taste the exquisitely light

Vintage Spot
THE SPOTTED CAT MUSIC CLUB: EST. 2000

If you are on your way to the Old New Orleans Rum Distillery, stop first at the Spotted Cat Music Club. It's just an old hole in the wall in an even older building, but if you are a true jazz aficionado, you might want to venture down to 623 Frenchmen Street to the quintessential jazz club in the heart of the historic Faubourg Marigny District. The Frenchmen Street area is said to be the locals' version of Bourbon Street. This sweet spot is the ultimate place to experience blues, jazz, gypsy swing, and traditional jazz. Jazz enthusiasts have discovered "The Cat" and it can get very crowded during festivals and on game days. The space gets very tight and you may have to dance in place, but drinks are cheap and there's no cover charge. Whether you are looking for blues, jazz, Latin or a mix of these styles, be ready for a great experience. The space is intimate and the energy is contagious. The venue is decorated with colorful signage, mirrors, and vintage motifs. The Spotted Cat is open on weekdays from 4 p.m. to 2 a.m. and weekends from 3 p.m. to 2 a.m. On a typical Sunday night you will be tapping your foot with some of the best musicians in the city. On Wednesday you can take swing lessons. Only cash (an ATM is on-site) is accepted. The club offers varieties of local Abita beer, serves no food, and does not take reservations. Check the website for a calendar of scheduled bands and events.

623 Frenchmen St.; (504) 943-3887;
spottedcatmusicclub.com

Crystal, a white rum used in daiquiris and mojitos. Also available at the tastings are two types of rum: Amber, aged in charred American oak for three years, and Cajun Spice, a blended New Orleans rum with chicory and a variety of spices. The distillery is working on a new variety of rum called Gingeroo. It is a pre-mixed beverage made with Old New Orleans rum. "We want to change the perception of ready-to-drink cocktails," says Jason Coleman, manager at Old New Orleans Rum Distillery, in an interview with My House NOLA titled "Drink Up: Old New Orleans Rum." "We like to say that we make the cocktail just like any other bartender—we just use a 500-gallon shaker," he adds.

The distillery is open 6 days a week, Monday through Friday from 9 a.m. to 5 p.m. and Saturday from 1 to 5:30 p.m. Tours of the distillery are offered Monday through Friday at noon, 2 p.m., and 4 p.m. and Saturday at 2 p.m. and 4 p.m. You can show up at the distillery—no reservations required. The guy behind the bar offered me a beer as I entered the low doorway, and I wasn't even taking the tour. "We have some of the best rum around," he exclaimed. But I had to pass; I was working. Complimentary shuttle transportation from the French Quarter is available, but you need to call in advance to reserve free van pickup at designated times at either the Erin Rose Bar at 811 Conti Street or at the Organic Banana at 1100 N. Peters Street, both in the French Quarter. You can also take a taxi (approximately a 10-minute ride from the French Quarter), and if you are driving your car there is ample free parking. The website displays a location map under the "Times and Location" section of the "Tour the Distillery" tab.

The distillery is definitely off the beaten path, but the tour is quite educational and you get to taste some great rum. Try the King Cake Cocktail with aged Cajun Spiced Rum amped up with cinnamon, nutmeg, ginger, and cloves.

For some great rum recipes you can go to oldneworleansrum .com/recipes/. Here's a Streetcar #9 cocktail recipe for you:

1 teaspoon cinnamon
1 teaspoon sugar
lemon wedge
2 ounces Old New Orleans Cajun Spice Rum
1 ounce Cointreau orange liqueur
2 teaspoons fresh lemon juice
lemon twist for garnish

1. Combine the cinnamon and sugar on a small plate. Run the lemon wedge around the edge of a martini glass, and then dip the glass in the cinnamon-sugar mixture to coat.

2. Combine the remaining ingredients in an ice-filled cocktail shaker. Shake vigorously for 10 seconds, strain into the cocktail glass, and garnish with the lemon twist and a dash of cinnamon.

The distillery cautions that an Old New Orleans Rum Streetcar #9 "ain't your average trolley." Be careful how many you drink or you may feel like you were run over by one the next day.

OUR LADY OF GUADALUPE CHURCH

411 N. RAMPART ST. • NEW ORLEANS, LA 70112

(504) 525-1551 • JUDESHRINE.COM

There Are Saints for All Causes!

*I*f you find yourself in New Orleans on a Saturday afternoon or Sunday morning and you want to really feel like a native . . . then you must go to church. In New Orleans streets are named after saints, religious statues adorn public parks, and private front yards and religious holidays are reasons for prestigious social events.

Services are still held today at Our Lady of Guadalupe, the oldest church in New Orleans. Back in 1826, it was built as a burial church for New Orleanians dying of yellow fever. Many believed the disease was spread from dead bodies, so funeral services at the St. Louis Cathedral were forbidden. The small, but sturdy Mortuary Chapel was built on Rampart Street near the cemeteries then in use. The humble structure was designed with a triple-arched façade and a small belfry. The first funeral in the mortuary chapel was on All Saints' Day, 1827. No one was allowed in the chapel, except the priests, altar boys, and pallbearers carrying the coffin. No pews were installed and families observed the service through the open doors of the church.

By 1841, the funeral chapel was also serving as a chapel of ease to the St. Louis Cathedral, for marriage ceremonies and baptisms, but it gradually lost its importance and was temporarily abandoned from 1856 to 1865. Near the end of the Civil War, the chapel was reopened to serve the spiritual needs of returning Confederate soldiers, only to be abandoned again from 1868 to 1873. Some have called the funeral church, ironically, "the church that would not die."

When waves of immigration swept into the area in the 1870s, the church now serving Italian immigrants was renamed St. Anthony of Padua Chapel. Thirty years later, the church came under the Spanish Dominican Order, who promptly removed the belfry's dome and added a steeple. By 1915, the City of New Orleans had expanded far beyond its original borders and the chapel's proximity to the notorious Storyville, the "red light" district, led to rumors that it would be sold. But that was not to happen.

In 1918, the Oblates of Mary Immaculate took charge of the St. Louis Cathedral, St. Mary's Italian Church, and the St. Anthony of Padua Chapel. The chapel sat abandoned for 3 years until 1921, when it was cleared of broken plaster and debris and restored for a Spanish-speaking Catholic congregation; it was now called Our Lady of Guadalupe. Statues soon adorned the church and devotees came in to pray to their favorite saints, including St. Expedite (more on him below). In 1940, the infamous Storyville became the Federal Iberville Housing Project, and over 800 families moved into the area. Most of them would be parishioners at Our Lady of Guadalupe.

Devotion to St. Jude Thaddeus, the patron for impossible cases, started in 1935. An authenticated relic of St. Jude was donated to the church and a small statue of St. Jude was placed in a side niche. For the last 50 years the church has been celebrated as a shrine dedicated to St. Jude. Our Lady of Guadalupe Church is also the official chapel of the New Orleans Police and Fire Departments.

New Orleans has a saint for every cause. St. Expedite, long the saint for urgent causes and quick solutions, has become the favorite saint of computer techies. St. Expedite's following has grown despite his unsanctioned sainthood status. One legend has it that the Chapel of Our Lady of Guadalupe requested a statue of the Virgin Mary from France. But when the ship arrived in port, it had two crates addressed to the church. In the first was the eagerly awaited statue of Mary. The second crate was imprinted EXPEDITE and inside was a statue of a Roman centurion. Why the statue was sent to New Orleans is still a mystery. You can see this nearly 200-year-old statue in the Chapel of Our Lady of Guadalupe, said to be the only Catholic Church in North America to contain a statue of St. Expedite.

Catholic ritual and voodoo often commingle in New Orleans and St. Expedite is venerated by voodoo practitioners who seek favors. Believers say St. Expedite prefers fresh flowers, a glass of rum, or a slice of pound cake in exchange for granting requests.

But don't get too overzealous—the Missionary Oblates of Mary Immaculate forbid these offerings to be placed at the feet of St. Expedite. (You can leave gifts in his name at voodoo priestess Marie Laveau's grave, next door in St. Louis Cemetery No. 1.) St. Expedite is very involved in the community and is often mentioned in the personal columns of the local newspaper as public thanks for answered prayers. If you go to Our Lady of Guadalupe Church you will see locals standing at his statue, rubbing his feet, petitioning for miracles.

Services at Our Lady of Guadalupe are on Sunday at 7:30, 9:30, and 11:30 a.m., 1:30 p.m. (Spanish), and 6 p.m.; weekdays at 7 a.m. and noon; Saturday at 7 a.m. and 4 p.m. (Saturday Vigil).

You can stop by the St. Jude Gift Shop to buy candles, rosaries, medals, crosses, statues, and prayer cards, Monday through Saturday from 9 a.m. to 5 p.m. and Sunday from 7 a.m. to 6 p.m.

PAT O'BRIEN'S

718 ST. PETER ST. • NEW ORLEANS, LA 70116

(504) 525-4823 / (800) 597-4823 • PATOBRIENS.COM

Sure, You Can Keep the Glass!

Y ou must put Pat O'Brien's at the top of your to-do list. Millions of people have wet their whistle here in this very old establishment.

Pat O'Brien's is housed in one of three 18th-century buildings that stand together in a row. Specific addresses and owners of these surviving structures are hard to trace. Official documents have mixed and intertwined the French, Creole, Spanish, and English names. But there's no doubt that this trio of historic structures dates back to the 1700s when New Orleans was a thriving French city.

The property was first owned by Francois Collell in 1791. Over 150 years later B. H. "Pat" O'Brien needed a bigger building for his Mr. O'Brien's Club Tipperary, and in 1942 he bought the present building with its old bricked carriageway entrance and aged slate flooring. In the late 1970s, the Oechsners bought the business. The company now has four independently owned franchises, two restaurants, an online catalog, and a bottling plant. The popular bar complex on St. Peter Street has five bars and an outdoor dining courtyard.

You can dance in the aisles to dueling twin baby grand pianos in the Piano Lounge or relax in the courtyard, dazzled by the flaming water fountain. Pat O'Brien's claims to sell more alcohol per square foot than any other establishment in the country. Its signature drink, the Hurricane, became popular in the 1940s, after debuting at the 1939 World's Fair in New York. During World War II, whiskey, bourbon, and scotch were in short supply because grains and sugars were sent to the troops fighting abroad. In New Orleans there was, however,

easy access to rum from the Caribbean Islands. To create more demand for his rum products, it is said that an eager liquor salesman combined light rum, dark rum, fruit juices, grenadine, and sugar, then shook the ingredients with crushed ice and added a cherry and orange slice garnish. Pat O'Brien serves the fruity rum concoction in a glass shaped like a hurricane lamp. Today the Pat O'Brien's Hurricane glass is a highly coveted city souvenir, and most locals own at least one. (I own two!) One patron quoted on the bar's website claims that the glass can hold "exactly $10.00 in pennies." Drinks, such as the Cyclone and Tornado, in their own uniquely shaped glasses, are also menu options.

New Orleanians celebrate every type of event at Pat O'Brien's, from birthday celebrations to bachelorette parties. When is the best time to visit? On Mardi Gras Day, Pat O'Brien's offers drink and food specials all day long. In the middle of March, you can mingle with Irish locals (and Irish wannabes) at the annual St. Patrick's Day celebration. Can't get to the city until April? Don't worry. Pat O'Brien's will be serving its signature "ass kicking" Hurricanes during the famous French Quarter Fest. In May you can join in the Annual Kentucky Derby Party where mint juleps are half price! If you choose to visit New Orleans during the steamy days of summer, don't miss the Independence Day $3 Rainbow drink special. In August you can participate in the annual Bar Golf Open. You don't really need to be good at this sport because you won't be playing any golf! You will be joining a golf-themed bar crawl with drinking games at bars representing "holes" on a golf course. If you happened to have missed the St. Patrick's Day celebration way back in March . . . the Luck of the Irish is with you! The annual Halfway to St. Patrick's Day Party is every September. On October 31, the party gears up with a Halloween Costume Contest. Purple People Eater drinks are $3 all night! Pat O'Brien's is said to be haunted, so don't be surprised if you feel the presence of unearthly patrons. One of the traditional fun nights at Pat O'Brien's is Christmas Day night and a week later, you can wave goodbye to the old year and ring in the new year. Enjoy a delicious buffet, live music, champagne toast at midnight, and a great view of fireworks over the Mississippi River.

Pat O'Brien's bars open at noon, Monday–Thursday, and 10 a.m., Friday–Sunday. The Piano Lounge show begins at 6 p.m., Monday–Thursday and 2 p.m., Friday–Sunday. The Courtyard Restaurant offers outdoor dining, rain or shine, in a lush tropical garden (all ages are welcomed, but you must be 21 to enter the bar) and is open daily from 11 a.m. to 10 p.m. For a unique appetizer order the Alligator Bites and wash 'em down with a local Abita Amber beer.

Many celebrities have enjoyed Pat O's: Richard Burton and Elizabeth Taylor, Billy Joel, Willie Nelson, Speaker of the House Tip O'Neill, and Sean Connery. Recent visitors include Dick Butkus, the Mannings of football fame, and country music star Kenny Chesney. Shelly Oechsner Waguespack, vice president, likes when celebrities visit, but says on the Pat O'Brien's website, "Even though millions of people visit every year, locals are the reason the doors stay open," You shouldn't miss this local watering hole experience either.

PRESERVATION HALL

726 ST. PETER ST. • NEW ORLEANS, LA 70116

(504) 522-2841 • PRESERVATIONHALL.COM

Enjoy Old-Time New Orleans
Jazz at Its Best

*A*re you ready to kick off your heels and enjoy the music? How about listening to some traditional New Orleans jazz, one of America's homegrown art forms? The best spot in town to enjoy this awesome music is Preservation Hall, a small venue in the French Quarter where seasoned and up-and-coming jazz musicians share their souls with the world. Put on your happy feet and get ready to be entertained by some of the greatest musicians in the country!

Preservation Hall had its beginnings in the 1950s when art gallery owner Larry Borenstein invited jazz musicians to perform "rehearsal sessions" in his gallery. The public was invited. Jazz greats such as George Lewis, Sweet Emma Barrett, Billie and De De Pierce, and Punch Miller were happy to oblige. When the jazz crowds overtook his gallery business, Borenstein moved his gallery next door and passed the operation of the nightly jazz performances to tuba player Allan Jaffe.

Preservation Hall officially opened in 1961, but in a city that celebrates history, it's worth noting that the building where these jazz greats have continued to congregate for over 50 years has been an integral part of the city's past. Historic documents show that Don Antonio Faisendieu purchased this property from Don Geronimo Gros around 1750 and changed the previously private residence into a tavern called Faisendieu's Posada. The bar became a popular New Orleans entertainment nightspot. But its reputation eventually waned, and in the years following the tavern's closing, the building housed several, more respectable, establishments: a small inn, a photographer's studio, and Borenstein's art gallery.

Preservation Hall is the premier showplace for New Orleans music. Writer Vanessa Franko says Preservation Hall provides "a place where the flavor of local jazz musicians can simmer and grow into part of the New Orleans cultural gumbo." Aged, cloudy portraits of early musicians hang on the ancient bricked walls of the hall and the lush tropical courtyard is protected from outside street traffic by an ornate wrought-iron gate. After taking over the jazz rehearsals, Jaffe founded Preservation Hall. After his death, son Benjamin, graduate of Oberlin Conservatory, took over as musical director. Benjamin plays bass and tuba with the band, while tending to the website and working on the group's small record label. "Our role is to nourish and help protect the community that gave birth to one of our great American art forms, something that is truly American," says Ben Jaffe on the Preservation Hall website. He has updated its musical repertoire by bringing in younger musicians with fresh ideas. His collaborative efforts with Tom Waits, My Morning Jacket, and the Del McCoury Bluegrass Band resulted in a sellout 50th anniversary concert at Carnegie Hall in 2012.

Erle Stanley Gardner, author of the well-known Perry Mason detective novels, lived in an apartment above Preservation Hall. One of his stories, "The Case of the Singing Skirt" (1959), was dedicated to Nicholas M. Chetta, MD, a former New Orleans coroner. Mementos in the hall include a funeral wreath mounted in the carriageway that marked the 2006 passing of banjoist and last founding member of the original band, Narvin Kimball, who died at age 97.

Today Preservation Hall presents intimate acoustic jazz concerts 350 nights a year. In this small, austere, no-frills venue, you are treated to authentic jazz music by legendary band members who play well into their senior years. The creaky stage floor seems to come to life as the music begins and visitors and locals stomp their feet and clap their hands to the rhythm of the beat. You won't mind at all that there are no amplifiers, no microphones and . . . no air-conditioning! It's all part of the ambience.

Preservation Hall supports the Preservation Hall Foundation, a community outreach that offers free concerts for school children. "As a musical component to our community we make sure that our music

is an active part of our community," says resident sousaphonist Ronell Johnson on the hall's website. Preservation Hall bands regularly tour the country and hold concerts around the world.

At night, every night, Preservation Hall fills to capacity. You can get reserved seats for some concerts, such as the Preservation Hall Ball, but most seating is first-come, first-served. Lines form outside on the pavement in front of the building. Live traditional New Orleans jazz is played nightly at 8, 9, and 10 p.m. All ages are welcome. You can subscribe to the monthly newsletter for updates on tours and concerts on the Preservation Hall website at preservationhall.com. The band's first album of all-original material in its five-decade history is titled *That's It* and can be downloaded on iTunes, Amazon, or Barnes & Noble.

Jaffe advises all of you to let your hair down and embrace the "festive" feel of the local culture. "New Orleans jazz is a living and breathing experience," Jaffe says in an interview for the *Press Enterprise*. So get on down to St. Peter Street, stand in line, and make some new friends. Once you get into the hall, take out your fan (if you must), but get ready to enjoy some authentic New Orleans jazz. You can stomp, clap in time, and even dance with the person next to you, if you can find the space.

ROCK 'N' BOWL

3000 S. CARROLLTON AVE. • NEW ORLEANS, LA 70118

(504) 861-1700 • ROCKNBOWL.COM

Family Bowling Night Will Never Be the Same!

*I*n the 1940s if you wanted to bowl the night away in New Orleans, Mid-City Lanes was the place to go. You had to climb up the stairs of a creaking building in a small commercial mall to get to the lanes, but that was part of the bowling alley's ambience.

When John Blancher took over Mid-City Lanes in 1988, he was determined to increase the popularity of bowling in a city where music and fun were the soul of every activity. His dream came to life on November 2, 1989, when Johnny J & the Hitmen performed live at his bowling alley. Subsequently, the lanes became known as Rock 'n' Bowl. In the mid 1990s, Rock 'n' Bowl expanded to the ground floor adding another bar and stage for live shows beneath the bowling alley, called "Bowl Me Under."

Rock 'n' Bowl was one of the first businesses to reopen in Mid-City after Hurricane Katrina hit in August of 2005. The ground floor suffered severe flood damage, but the second-floor bowling alley and main music stage survived the high winds and 7 feet of floodwater. The upstairs remained open during reconstruction of the gutted ground floor and the building got a new façade. The entire venue reopened in December 2005.

When the building's lease option came up for renewal in 2009, Blancher decided to make a move and bought a large building just 11 blocks away. He designed a new, modern bowling facility, the first bowling venue to be built in Orleans Parish in decades, around a performance stage and dance floor. But he kept artifacts

from the bowling alley's illustrious past. Parts of artist and "gypsy jazz" guitarist Tony Green's giant New Orleans street scenes were dismantled and moved to the new location. Green's nostalgic murals depicted Pelican Stadium, a neighborhood bar with a red Jax beer sign, and a young Pete Fountain leading Professor Longhair, bassist Jim Singleton, and Green himself on guitar. Green's street scene was too big to fit through the doors so it was cut lengthwise, but even halved, the mural endured an awkward trek down the stairs. The Pete Fountain band section got wedged in the doorway; doors and hinges had to be removed. "It would have been a real pity to have this little slice of New Orleans life tossed into a dumpster," Green said in an interview for the *New Orleans Times-Picayune* ("Watch: Rock 'n' Bowl Murals Move to Their New Home").

Other relics were toted down the street to the new venue. Business as usual meant taking the old sandwich-making machine and the huge beer cooler. Blancher kept the wood from lanes 17 and 18 to slice up for table tops and souvenir squares. "It's tough to decide what to keep," Blancher said in the *Times-Picayune* article. Since the move he has restored pieces of the old maple bar for his new venue's party rooms. One of his most prized possessions, the portrait of the Blessed Mother that had hung near the jukebox since Rock 'n' Bowl's beginnings was carried out in Blancher's arms as he left the building for the last time. The new Rock 'n' Bowl is just outside the Mid-City neighborhood limits, so the "Mid-City" had to be dropped, but the old "Mid-City Lanes" sign was rescued and can be seen on the new building.

The new venue officially opened on April 15, 2009, but not without some drama. It seems the state alcoholic beverage commission couldn't do its inspection until that morning and the liquor license, which must be physically posted, didn't arrive until 30 minutes before the doors were set to open.

Johnny J & the Hitmen, the rockabilly combo that had been the first to play at the original Rock 'n' Bowl in 1989, and saxophonist Derek Huston were on hand to christen the new venue. Owner John Blancher was so excited that he jumped atop the bar, grabbed a hula hoop, and began twisting.

Both natives and tourists, bowlers and non-bowlers, come to Rock 'n' Bowl to eat, drink, rock, and bowl to R&B, zydeco, Cajun music, rock, blues, and jazz. The club features many local musicians, such as Beau Jocque, Geno Delafose, Snooks Eaglin, the Zydeco Twisters, and Wild Magnolias.

New Orleans celebrities have endorsed the live music and bowling venue. According to NOLA.com, Harry Connick approves of the new Rock 'n' Bowl and New Orleans Jazz Fest producer Quint Davis laughingly said the new technology and classy hardwood floors are "almost too nice for New Orleans."

Rock 'n' Bowl sits in the heart of the city. It's a great place for food, fun, music, and bowling and at a bargain! There is no cover charge, except for special events. Bowling is open Monday–Thursday from 11:30 a.m. to midnight and Friday and Saturday from 11:30 a.m. to 2 a.m. Shoe rentals are $1, and shoe rentals are free for family bowling hours Monday–Thursday, from 11:30 a.m. to 4 p.m. Bowlers should check the Rock 'n' Bowl calendar online for Sunday availability. Lanes are $24 per hour with a maximum of six bowlers. At the Front Porch Grill you can enjoy a full bar, a variety of beers, and local delicacies such as Grilled Boudin Links, Duck Nachos, beignets, Fried Bread Pudding Po'boys, and Chicken Salad with Pepper Jelly Vinaigrette— each for $10 or less. Are you ready to Rock 'n' Bowl?

RODRIGUE STUDIO

732 ROYAL ST. • NEW ORLEANS, LA 70116
(504) 581-4244 • GEORGERODRIGUE.COM

Have You Heard of the Famous "Blue Dog?"

*T*he iconic Blue Dog artwork has been exhibited throughout the world. If you are visiting New Orleans you will see a lot of the Blue Dog, because this is where creative artist George Rodrigue spent much of his time. His gallery is on Royal Street, adjacent to the St. Louis Cathedral and overlooking St. Anthony's Gardens.

Before this space became the Rodrigue Studio, the building had been home to a very famous tea shop, the Bottom of the Cup Tea Room. And before that it was a rendezvous apartment where one of the most legendary New Orleans ghost stories began.

History has it that on the roof of this building, a young woman named Julie froze to death attempting to prove her love and loyalty to a well-to-do young man. Feeling pushed into a corner to propose marriage, creating an unlawful union between an aristocrat and a mixed-blood woman, the man made a promise to Julie that if she stayed on the roof of their third-room hideaway all night, he would defy the law and marry her. The young man felt confident that his impossible bargain would soon be forgotten. But Julie was determined to win the dare. As a winter ice storm blew in from the north, friends who had dropped by for whiskey and a game of cards stayed on. Toward dawn, the young man looked for Julie, and unable to find her . . . remembered his ultimatum. He rushed to the rooftop to find Julie's frozen dead body clinging to the chimney. The distraught young man despairingly took his own life.

By 1929 Wilhelmina Mullen had set up her tea shop and psychic business on the ground floor of Julie's building. A large, sepia-toned

photograph hung in the shop depicting women in flapper sheaths holding cups of tea and eagerly awaiting their turns to dash behind the velvet curtain in the rear of the shop to have their fortunes told. Since it was illegal to charge for telling someone's future, the tearoom gave free readings, but sold very expensive tea to make a profit. Julie's ghost, it is said, haunted the tearoom. She was known for spraying her magnolia perfume on women customers or fiddling with their hair. She also reportedly played jokes on the men who ventured into the tearoom. Otis Biggs, professional psychic and tearoom regular, has had many run-ins with the "Octoroon Mistress." She is always drumming her fingernails; he says in an interview with NOLA.com that they go, "click, click, on the table." As the years wore on, Mullen's daughter-in-law, Adele, took over the business. By 1975, Adele had stopped serving tea and began selling incense, books, cards, crystal balls, and voodoo dolls.

Today at this address, you will find the Rodrigue Studio. This space (along with an adjacent area at 730 Royal) is the art gallery of George Rodrigue, Louisiana native and creator of the beloved Blue Dog. This is a stop well worth your time. Rodrigue's various works featuring the Blue Dog are famous worldwide and the gallery holds a fantastic collection. Following his exhibition of *The Kingfish* in Paris, he was called the "Louisiana Rousseau" by *Le Figaro*. His portrait of Saints quarterback Drew Brees helped raise funds for Blue Dog Relief after Hurricane Katrina. The building is also a stop on the nightly New Orleans ghost tours where the story of Julie and her unrequited love is kept alive. It is said that her ghost still wanders the roof as she calls for her lover, especially on cold, icy nights. What's very strange is that in the mid 1980s, Rodrigue painted *A Night Alone* depicting this famous ghost story, and now his gallery is housed in this same building—the setting for the only painting Rodrigue ever created of the French Quarter. So eerie . . .

Be sure to check out Rodrigue's 40-foot Blue Dog in the Sheraton Hotel downtown and his 24-foot Blue Dog outdoor sculpture of steel, aluminum, and chrome on Veterans Highway.

When the art gallery moved to this Royal Street location in 2010, the Bottom of the Cup Tea Room moved to 327 Chartres. You can take a quick walk, about 4 blocks toward Canal Street, and browse through this legendary establishment that still employs some of the city's most famous psychics. Tea has been a favorite drink in New Orleans. Though coffee was a major import from the islands, many citizens still cling to their tea-drinking traditions. In past glory days, Creole mistresses in the French Quarter sipped tea as they entertained gentleman callers. When the Bottom of the Cup Tea Room originally opened in 1929, psychics would visit the tables of the fancy women drinking their tea, and read the tea leaves scattered in the bottom of the cup. Remember that large sepia photo of women waiting for their fortunes to be told that hung in the Royal Street shop? It was brought, lovingly, to the new location and hangs on the wall near the entrance. Gesturing toward the picture, owner Adele points out that one woman is pregnant. "That's my mother-in-law," Adele says, "She's carrying my husband, Tom." For more than 80 years the Bottom of the Cup has touted its reputation for reliable and authentic psychic readings. The shop carries unique items such as feng shui essentials, tarot cards, metaphysical books, religious figurines, pyramids, incense, pendulums, spheres, crystals, and crystal balls, and jewelry carved from a variety of minerals and semi-precious stones. Bottom of the Cup, open daily from 10 a.m. to 6 p.m., offers over a hundred varieties of the world's finest teas and tea accessories.

RUBENSTEINS

102 ST. CHARLES AVE. • NEW ORLEANS, LA 70130

(504) 581-6666 • RUBENSTEINSNEWORLEANS.COM

When Is a Men's Store Not Just a Men's Store?

When it's Rubensteins!

Hailed by many as the "Barney's New York store of the South," Rubensteins has been serving New Orleans residents and visitors of discriminating taste for more than 90 years! In fact, it was once a rite of passage for little New Orleans boys to get their first long pants and navy blazer from the big men's store downtown.

Morris Rubenstein was the son of Russian immigrants who owned a work-wear shop on Rampart Street. But Morris had bigger dreams; of course, those visions were rooted in the retail industry. In 1924, he opened Rubensteins Men's Store on Canal Street, near his family's dry goods business. His mission was to offer men's shirts, ties, handkerchiefs, and separate collars to an upscale clientele, while giving them unparalleled service and amenities.

Within 6 months, Morris was joined by his two brothers, Elkin and Sam, and the store's name was officially changed to Rubenstein Bros. By 1927, the brothers had leased a second building on Canal Street, but this space was abandoned 2 years later following the stock market crash. By 1937, post-Depression, the brothers were ready to expand again, this time taking over a corner building to make room for more furnishings and sportswear collections. Soon the legendary (still revolving) neon "Rubensteins" sign was placed on the corner of Canal Street and St. Charles Avenue, and you can see it today. Rubensteins was one of the first retail stores to introduce credit accounts and, because of a shortage of men's merchandise

163

during World War II, it added women's apparel. At the end of the war, with tens of thousands of male soldiers needing "civvies," women's apparel was discontinued.

The reputation of Rubensteins and its exclusive appeal spread far and wide, and by the end of the 1950s the store was not only carrying famous designer merchandise, purchased from the elite showrooms of New York, but was courted as an exclusive outlet for Ralph Lauren and other famous designers. Rubensteins still carries Ralph Lauren merchandise in its hallowed halls.

Staying ahead of the trend has been the hallmark of Rubensteins' success. In the late 1950s and early 1960s, the store introduced "Prep-wear" looks of the day that were featured in a new "stand-alone" area they called the Madison Shop. For this discerning customer, the Madison Shop had its own entrance off Canal Street. To attract and engage "walking-by" customers, Rubensteins began placing live mannequins, wearing London Fog apparel, in their store windows. The mannequins were a novelty as gawkers stopped to stare. The stunt apparently caused a sidewalk frenzy! Ben Jaffe, leader of the Preservation Hall Jazz Band, recalls that his father's generation wore shoes bought at Rubensteins as "a badge of honor and source of pride," according to the *New Orleans Advocate* in April 2014.

In the early 1970s Rubenstein family members redirected their energies toward capturing the younger shopper. They launched their own All American Jeans sportswear label. As an innovative spirit continued to push the store forward, Rubensteins became the first US store to carry clothing from the Italian designer Ermenegildo Zegna. Men from across the South would make the pilgrimage to New Orleans just to be fitted in his latest style. Even today, Rubensteins is a popular shopping mecca. Bryan Batt, former *Mad Men* actor and New Orleans native, says the unique clothing he has bought at Rubensteins has a nostalgic New Orleans feel to it.

You, too, can shop, or just meander through, Rubensteins. You will be glad you crossed over the streetcar tracks to get to the other side of Canal Street from the French Quarter. Today Rubensteins' reported sales are in excess of $5 million. The store has been recognized by *Esquire* magazine as a "Gold Standard Best of Class" retailer. As a longtime loyal customer of Rubensteins, I can tell you that while this family-owned store is known for changing its fashion styles

Vintage Spot

MEYER THE HATTER: EST. 1894

"Take off your hat," the King said to the Hatter. "It isn't mine," said the Hatter . . . "I keep them to sell," the Hatter added as an explanation; "I've none of my own. I'm a hatter."

Perhaps Sam Meyer was inspired by reading Lewis Carroll's *Alice's Adventures in Wonderland* when he started the little hat store on St. Charles Avenue in 1894. Whatever his motivation, it has certainly stood the test of time, outlasting its competition, overcoming the obstacles of subsequent "hatless" fashion cycles, and managing to inspire current generations to continue running the business.

You might doubt the sincerity of the claim "the largest hat store in the south" when you view the shop from the outside, but when you enter and see the mounds of hats stacked in every corner and crevice, you quickly understand and are reassured that you will find both your style and size.

Along with experienced and knowledgeable service, you will find every brand of hat you recognize, and many that you don't, such as Aegean, Biltmore, Akubra, Bailey, Dobbs, Capas, Resistol, Sunfari, Ozark, Barmah . . . need we go on? Buy a hat; your head will thank you!

120 St. Charles Ave.; (504) 525-1048; meyerthehatter.com

according to market trends, it has been its excellent customer service that has led to the longevity of its business. Rubensteins is still in its original location and although its selections and designer collections have expanded and been updated, its business approach to serving customers in search of quality and value has never faltered.

While clothes shopping might not be your first priority while visiting the Big Easy, Rubensteins should be on your list as a must-do item for a true New Orleans cultural experience. Your unique trip will start with Rubensteins' valet service out front, right at its entrance doors on the famous Canal Street (if you can accomplish the seemingly impossible feat of stopping anywhere along this busy

thoroughfare!). The store still offers custom-fitting and tailoring to its customers. And don't be surprised if you are greeted at the door by one of the Rubenstein family members as you enter their exquisite emporium of design and fashion, a courtesy not available today amid the hustle and bustle of most retail stores. Saints NFL football team co-owner Rita Benson LeBlanc in an interview for the *Advocate*, says the store exudes "masculine class" and is "a home for elegance . . . [with] a vibe of Southern charm and dashing men."

By the way, this is perhaps the only retail store in the city where you can find an in-house, fully furnished and staffed shoeshine stand. Now, that's class!

SAENGER THEATRE

1111 CANAL ST. • NEW ORLEANS, LA 70112

(504) 525-1052 • SAENGERNOLA.COM

Want to Feel like Royalty?

𝓘f you are in the mood for a great cultural experience, you won't find a better place to sit back and enjoy superior entertainment than the magnificent Saenger Theatre. This theater is a rare surviving example of the opulent theaters that sprang up in the country during the first three decades of the 20th century.

The newly restored theater sits proudly on Canal Street and is easily accessible by foot, car, bus, streetcar, or taxi from uptown, downtown or the French Quarter. Ravaged by Hurricane Katrina floodwaters in 2005, the theater finally reopened in its entire majestic splendor in 2013.

The past two seasons have brought notable productions to the expanded stage. If you can't get to New York City, seeing a Broadway play in the Saenger is the next best thing. Check out the online calendar for upcoming productions and get your tickets early. The Saenger is extremely popular with locals who nostalgically remember this icon of entertainment as an integral part of New Orleans life. Some noteworthy recent Broadway plays include *The Phantom of the Opera*, *The Book of Mormon*, *Mamma Mia!*, *Joseph and the Amazing Technicolor Dreamcoat*, and *Once*. Concerts by Celtic Woman, Melissa Etheridge, and John Mellencamp as well as performances by Cirque de Noel and the Moscow Ballet have graced the new Saenger stage.

It is easy to see why the Saenger has been called "The South's Grandest Theatre." The flamboyant production space was originally designed by Emile Weil for Julian Saenger in 1927, for the staggering price of $2.5 million. As you sit comfortably in the new plush seats,

SAENGER

SAENGER

SAENGER

THE NUTCRACKER SAT
MAMMA MIA JAN 13 TO 18
DWTS LIVE JANUARY 28
IN THE MOOD JANUARY 30

SAENGERNOLA.COM

GREAT RUSSIAN NUTCRACKER SATURDAY
MAMMA MIA JANUARY 13 THRU 18
DANCING WITH THE STARS LIVE JAN 28
IN THE MOOD 40 S MUSIC REVUE JAN 30

SEASON TICKETS   800 218 7469

you can't help but drift back to the theater's glory days when the Saenger was the flagship venue in the Saenger family's chain of 237 theaters across the Southeast. The February 5, 1927, opening of the Saenger Theatre was heralded by a celebratory parade down Canal Street and the morning and afternoon newspapers devoted entire special sections to the ribbon cutting. To add to the fanfare, the *Times-Picayune* published a 20-page special describing the theater's Renaissance interior as "an acre of seats in a garden of Florentine splendor." The palatial interior was designed as a 15th-century Italian courtyard and gardens and the recent renovation has stayed true to this design. Stylistic arches, columns, and decorative moldings are in lavish abundance. The theater's signature blue domed "sky" ceiling, complete with twinkling constellations of stars and subtle projections of clouds, reigns overhead and the original Greek and Roman statues of gods and goddesses fill recesses along the walls.

Within months after Hurricane Katrina's wrath, public support for the theater's renovation was organized. The $53 million project was interconnected with the revitalization of Canal Street and the New Orleans Central Business District in an effort to build up the entire area while transforming the theater into a first-class state-of-the-art performing arts venue.

Restoring the old theater was arduous. The building and its furnishings had become time-worn and dingy, and some of the theater's iconic motifs were missing entirely, such as the lobby's ornate crystal chandeliers. These had been sold off decades earlier to bring in money for repairs. The organizers' mission was to create an authentic renovation. Carpet designs and lighting fixtures were recreated from the original designs. "We're peeling it back to its original beauty," Cindy Connick, executive director of Canal Street Development Corp., says in an interview for NOLA.com. There were some surprises along the way. Several original chandeliers were discovered in a French Quarter antiques store and once again hang in the grand theater today. The restorers found the theater's original blueprints in an obscure closet and were able to confirm specific architectural motifs. All efforts were made to bring back the original glory of the theater and its entrance arcade as it was in 1920s. The theater also had a spectacular organ, called The Wonder Organ with 778 pipes that could replicate an array of sounds beyond the expected orchestral instrument emanations—from automobile horns to barnyard sounds. The organ has survived, but it was severely damaged by floodwaters and is in storage awaiting full restoration. It will be worth the wait when the organ is finally returned to its honored place in the Saenger Theatre.

The renovated Saenger Theatre opened its doors in September of 2013. The building, now owned by the city of New Orleans, has been equipped with a state-of-the-art theatrical system ensuring that the Saenger is the most technically advanced theater in the South and capable of handling touring Broadway shows, live concerts, and other large-draw events.

If you visit the city, look for the new marquee along Canal Street. When complete it will be an authentic replication of the original vertical 1927 sign. It's up to you to take advantage of the Saenger Theatre as both a living piece of history (it is on the National Register of Historic Places) and as a place to join locals for some great entertainment. For over 85 years the Saenger has served as "the" theater experience for most New Orleanians as well as for many folks throughout the region.

SAZERAC BAR & GRILL

123 BARONNE ST. • NEW ORLEANS, LA 70112

(504) 648-1200 • THEROOSEVELTNEWORLEANS.COM

Want to Have a Drink in the Opulent 1940s Style?

*D*uring the 1830s pharmacist Antoine Peychaud ran a small apothecary on Royal Street. In the evenings he enjoyed mixing drinks for his friends who gathered at the pharmacy after hours. He served his concoctions in a *coquetier*, a French egg cup. The tradition caught on and as people began to talk about the coquetier, they pronounced the word in the French manner as "cock-tay" and eventually, imbibers began to slur the word. And so, the first, mixed-spirits "cocktail" was born and it happened right here in New Orleans. The title of "first cocktail" in the US is given to the mixture of Peychaud's house-brewed bitters and Sazerac-de-Forge et Fils brandy. In area coffee houses (Victorian euphemism for drinking establishments) the drink became known simply as a Sazerac and was popular among the city's elite, including politicians, merchants, and wealthy gentlemen. Today it is the official drink of the Krewe of Rex, king of Mardi Gras.

If you choose to stay at The Roosevelt, you will be sleeping in a room steeped in history. The original, six-story Grunewald Hotel was built in 1893 by Bavarian-born businessman Louis Grunewald. The lavish hotel opened to wide public acclaim just in time to herald in the 1894 Mardi Gras season. Near the hustle and bustle of Canal Street, the Grunewald was a centerpiece of the city's entertainment scene. When expansion was inevitable, adjoining property was procured and at the stroke of midnight on New Year's Eve 1907, a 400-room, 14-story addition opened to exuberant fanfare. The new addition offered fine

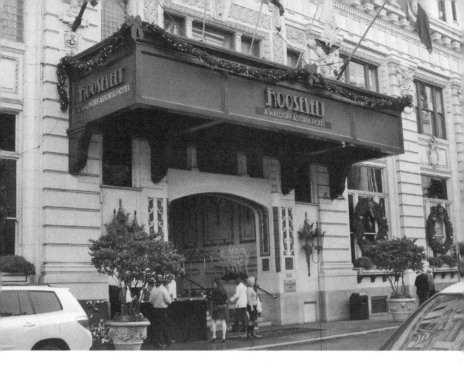

dining on glass-topped tables in The Cave, considered the country's first nightclub. This space was designed as a grotto with waterfalls, stalactites, and statues of nymphs. Revues and variety shows, lasting well into the early morning hours, were presented nightly. To see the remaining evidence of the original Grunewald Hotel, go out to the pavement in front of The Roosevelt Hotel's Baronne Street entrance. Hold on to your hat and look up above the present marquee. There embossed in stone you can see "The Grunewald Hotel."

In 1923, Grunewald sold the hotel to the Vacarro Group; the hotel was renamed to honor Theodore Roosevelt and his efforts to build the Panama Canal, which had greatly benefited the city's business interests. The hotel began elaborately decorating its block-long lobby for the Christmas season. If you plan to be in New Orleans during Christmas, be sure to view the gorgeous decorations of this long-standing tradition.

The Roosevelt Hotel era saw some new beginnings. On December 31, 1935, the Blue Room opened. Any New Orleanian with anything to celebrate booked a reservation at the Blue Room and the most famous entertainers of the time—including Louis Armstrong, Cab Calloway, Jack Benny, Glenn Miller, Tommy Dorsey, and Guy Lombardo—performed there. In 1949 The Sazerac Bar opened next

door to The Roosevelt's majestic front entrance, serving cocktails to both men and women, having abolished its "men only" house rule. Women flocked to The Sazerac Bar and their rush to be waited on at the bar became known as Storming the Sazerac. In celebration of the storming of the bar by women, this historical cultural change is re-created every year with events that include period costumes and vintage libations. The bar became so popular that it was moved to its current location inside the gilded hotel, just off the main lobby. Nine US presidents have stayed at The Roosevelt, as well as the King of Rock and Roll, Elvis Presley, during the filming of *King Creole* in 1957.

In 1965, the hotel was sold to the Swig family, owners of the Fairmont San Francisco, who changed its name to the Fairmont New Orleans. The Sazerac Restaurant featuring waiters in black tie and tableside preparations opened. The old coffee house storefront became Bailey's, which offered casual dining 24 hours a day.

Unfortunately, Hurricane Katrina extensively damaged the Fairmont New Orleans and the hotel was closed. Two years later it was sold to First Class Hotels, to be one of Hilton's premium hotels in its Waldorf Astoria Collection chain. The entire hotel was completely renovated and restored to its former magnificence with an embellished nod to its grand era of the 1930s and 1940s. But best of all, upon reopening the hotel in 2009, the name of the hotel became once again "The Roosevelt," the name it had held from 1923 to 1965.

The Sazerac Bar was restored to its original 1940s look. You can definitely feel the splendor of the "gilded age" in the opulent furnishings. The 45-foot bar is spectacular; rich African walnut paneling gives off a dark, sultry glow, art deco motifs have been restored, and Paul Ninas murals adorn the walls. The bar is still known for its Sazerac cocktail. It's made a little differently from the original Peychaud recipe because it uses rye instead of Sazerac-de-Forge at Fils brandy. Today, 2 ounces of rye whiskey is mixed with three to four dashes of bitters, some simple syrup, a touch of Herbsaint, an anise liqueur, and topped off with a twist of lemon peel. Bartenders are proud of the long heritage of this drink and mix their Sazerac cocktails with flamboyant style. After coating the glass with anise, they shake off the excess with a flourish and a dramatic toss of the glass.

Today you can enjoy the authentic Sazerac cocktail in the historic Sazerac Bar in one of New Orleans's oldest hotels.

ST. AUGUSTINE CHURCH

1210 GOVERNOR NICHOLLS ST. • NEW ORLEANS, LA 70116

(504) 525-5934 • STAUGUSTINECATHOLICCHURCH

-NEWORLEANS.ORG

Say a Prayer, Light a Candle, and Sing Along

*L*ooking for an authentic New Orleans religious experience? Want to hear some true grass roots gospel music? Then St. Augustine Church in the oldest African-American Catholic parish in the US is the place to be! The church sits in the Tremé neighborhood, made famous by the HBO series, *Tremé*, that ran from 2010 to 2013, and depicted New Orleanians rebuilding their lives after Hurricane Katrina.

According to the African American Registry website, the property that the church sits on was part of a tilery and brickyard built in 1720 by The Company of the Indies in the province of New Orleans, just 2 years after the city was founded. In 1731 the Moreau family bought the property for a plantation site and in 1775 the land came into the possession of Julie Moreau, a freed slave. Frenchman Claude Tremé married Julie Moreau and took lawful title of her property; the land became known as the Claude Tremé Plantation. The Tremés subdivided parts of the property and sold the lots to free people of color and others pouring into the area, especially Haitians fleeing the bloody revolution of 1791. Some of the property found its way into the hands of the Ursuline sisters, who, in the late 1830s, donated the corner property for the construction of a church petitioned by the free people of color living in the area. The parish was founded in 1841 and St. Augustine Church was dedicated on October 9, 1842.

Architecture buffs should know that the church was designed by J. N. B. de Pouilly, the French architect who worked on the much

Vintage Spot

THE BACKSTREET CULTURAL MUSEUM: EST. 1999

When you are ready for some local folklore, schedule a visit to The Backstreet Cultural Museum in the Tremé neighborhood of historic Faubourg Marigny, home to many skilled 18th-century artisans and "gens de couleur libre" or free blacks of African, Haitian, and Cuban origin. The museum was at one time the Blandin Funeral Home, an important institution to the local people and a landmark for jazz musicians and jazz funerals. Businesses on this part of St. Claude Avenue have had to change their letterhead because the street has been recently renamed in honor of Henriette DeLille, a local African-American nun up for canonization by the Roman Catholic Church.

The Backstreet Cultural Museum was founded in 1999 by Sylvester Francis, who has been photographing processions at black funerals since 1980. He will likely be your guide when you visit the museum and explain to you all about the century-old traditions of the Mardi Gras marching Indians. You can also see some of their extravagant costumes. Documentaries of African-American traditions such as the Mardi Gras Indians, jazz funerals, and Social Aid & Pleasure clubs are available for viewing. If you ask Mr. Sylvester, he can tell you where to go to experience an authentic Social Aid & Pleasure Club second-line. A second-line is a dance, single file, where members parade and gyrate in color-coordinated ensembles (including even the color of their shoes) to the energetic music of marching bands. The museum is open Tuesday—Saturday, from 10 a.m. to 5 p.m. Admission is $8.

1116 St. Claude Ave. (recently renamed Henriette DeLille St.); (504) 522-4806; backstreetmuseum.org

more famous St. Louis Cathedral just a few blocks over. One thing you will want to note about the church is its pews. At the time the church was built, it was the custom to charge pew fees to parishioners who wanted the privilege of sitting and kneeling in their designated pews.

This was a means of bringing in money to manage church business. The free people of color were entitled to buy their pews in the new church for their families. They also began buying pews for some of the less fortunate of the faithful: slaves who couldn't afford a place to sit. When the few whites in the area, mostly recent immigrants, heard about this, they felt that their place in the church hierarchy was being threatened and began buying up the pews. Thus began the "War of the Pews." The contest was ultimately won by the free people of color, who bought three times as many pews as the white folks. They bought pews flanking both sides of the center aisle, resulting in the most integrated congregational church seating in the country. As you look around the church imagine the congregation of 1842: one long row of free people of color, one row of whites with a smattering of immigrants, and two side rows full of slaves.

Whether Catholic or not, you can attend a service at St. Augustine Church. Sunday mass is at 10 a.m. Typically mass lasts nearly 2 hours, but no one cares if you come late or leave early. Those who have attended a Sunday service at the church say the inspiring music really makes you "get your praise on!" Others comment on the welcoming spirit and congenial atmosphere of the regular churchgoers.

The church also hosts the annual Jazz Mass, held in conjunction with the Satchmo Summer Jazz Festival that celebrates Louis Armstrong's birthday. If you plan to go to the festival, you should attend mass at St. Augustine's. Get to the church early to get a seat or else you will be praying for a place to sit halfway through the service. After mass is over, the band that was inside the church marches out to the street and is joined by several waiting bands and musical groups. Then everyone second-line dances to the vibrant music all the way to Louis Armstrong Park and from there to the festival site at the Old Mint Museum.

You can take a tour of St. Augustine Church, which is part of the African American Heritage Trail for historic sites of cultural significance in Louisiana. This honor was bestowed on the church by Lieutenant Governor Mitch Landrieu in 2008. To arrange a tour call the Rectory at (504) 525-5934.

If you explore St. Augustine's on your own, be sure to look for the Tomb of the Unknown Slave. This shrine, erected in 2004, is built of old crosses salvaged from derelict gravesites, rusty iron chains, and slave shackles. According to the memorial's plaque, this shrine "honors all slaves buried throughout the United States and those slaves in particular who lie beneath the ground of Tremé in unmarked, unknown graves." The plaque continues, "St. Augustine Church sits astride the blood, sweat, tears and some of the mortal remains of unknown slaves and local American Indian slaves who either met with fatal treachery, and were therefore buried quickly and secretly, or were buried hastily and at random because of yellow fever and other plagues."

Some of the more famous parishioners of St. Augustine Church have been Homer Plessy, early civil rights activist of the Supreme Court case *Plessy v. Ferguson*, and "Tootie" Montana, "Chief of Chiefs" of the Mardi Gras Indians.

You are fortunate to have the opportunity to experience the living history of St. Augustine Church. After Hurricane Katrina, the archdiocese decided to close down the struggling church and its parish activities due to a decrease in support. The parishioners barricaded themselves in the church's rectory as a demonstration against closure. After 2 weeks, parishioners and church officials agreed on a compromise that included procuring outside funding. A documentary covering the protest called *Shake the Devil Off* increased publicity for the parishioners' efforts to keep the church open. Subsequently, St. Augustine Church received a $75,000 grant from the National Trust for Historic Preservation and American Express. In 2009, the archdiocese took St. Augustine Church off its closure list.

THE ST. CHARLES AVENUE STREETCAR

ST. CHARLES AVE. • NEW ORLEANS, LA 70119

(504) 248-3900 • NORTA.COM

Riding in the City of New Orleans . . .

When someone says "trolley," think San Francisco. When someone says "streetcar," think New Orleans.

For more than 150 years, the St. Charles streetcar line has been clanging up and down the grand avenue of the Garden District. This gives it the distinction of being the world's oldest, continuously operating streetcar in the world. "Riding the line" through the stately oaks of St. Charles Avenue offers more than just a convenience from bustling traffic; it affords passengers breathtaking views of stately mansions, prestigious schools and universities, historic restaurants, and convenient stop-offs at Audubon Zoo, Commander's Palace, or Camellia Grill.

Seriously, where else in the world can you ride in scenic comfort for 13.1 miles and pay only $1.25? Even more amazing is that you can ride the entire streetcar system (multiple lines throughout the city) all day with a Jazzy Pass for $3! Children under 2 ride free and senior citizens ride for 40 cents. You gotta love it!

All the details you need to plan your streetcar trip can be found at norta.com. You can find time schedules, complete maps of streetcar lines and destinations, and a brief history of the city's streetcar system.

The "Desire" streetcar line, a route that included Bourbon Street, the French Quarter, and its namesake, Desire Street, stopped operating in 1948, but the streetcar's legacy can be found in Tennessee Williams's provocative play *A Streetcar Named Desire*. Because of the play's international prominence, visitors flock to the city each year to celebrate the playwright and the iconic French Quarter settings. The Tennessee Williams Literary Festival, now in its 29th year, is held every March in venues throughout the city.

If you stay in or around the French Quarter, you can catch the Canal Street line and ride up and down one of the broadest main streets in America, some 170 feet wide in most places. The streetcar can take you from the Mississippi River at one end of Canal Street to the Joy Theater at the other end.

The St. Charles line intersects along this route and you can transfer for a quick jaunt to the uptown district. Don't be afraid to get off and back on the streetcar as you sway along St. Charles Avenue (transfers are only 25 cents each or get the $3 all-day pass).

There's a lot to see and do as you wander and meander the side streets. Notice how the sprawling mansions back up to old, sometimes dilapidated, servants' quarters, or try to spot the quaint "shotgun" houses (narrow homes, one-room wide, where one room leads into the next are called shotgun houses because a bullet fired in the front door could depart out the back door without hitting a single door, wall, or piece of furniture). You can venture over to Lafayette Cemetery and wander down the rows of above-ground vaults or stop at some of the local eateries offering French, Spanish, and Cajun cuisine.

Here's a sample agenda for a day's outing. Catch the St. Charles streetcar on Canal Street at the corner of Carondelet Street, travel through the downtown business section, and then cross Loyola Avenue where you can catch a glimpse of the Superdome. By this time you could have already stopped and eaten, most certainly at Mother's Restaurant on Poydras for an early breakfast! Next you will round Lee Circle where the General stands proudly on a grand pedestal some 60 feet high. You have now been sitting for at least 10 minutes, so it's time to make a stop. You can get off here and walk a block to visit both the Civil War and the National World War II Museums.

Back on the streetcar, you are headed up St. Charles Avenue through the Garden District. Palatial old-world mansions, magnificent and timeless, seem to dominate the area. Some of the mansions are now businesses or hotels, but as you travel farther along the line, you will begin to understand why this area has been described as "The Jewel of America's Grand Avenues." If you want to grab a pressed po'boy for lunch, stop at The Grocery (with the inscription atop the

entrance door: "We are not a grocery, but serve good food"). You can eat outside and view all the goings-on at The Columns Hotel, a luxurious hotel where guests lounge on the front veranda to watch the world go by. If you want a more exquisite lunch, then you can stop at Commander's Palace for their daily special. Soon the meticulously maintained private residences and lavish hotels give way to the impressive colleges of Loyola and Tulane with grand sweeping entrances and towering cathedral-like buildings.

By the time you reach Audubon Park and Zoo on your left, you will have spied some shotgun houses and smaller neighbor parks. When you reach the wide bend in the Mississippi River, you will have arrived in P-Town in the Riverbend section of town and the beginning of Carrollton Avenue. Here you can indulge in a pecan waffle at Camellia Grille, a popular Sunday morning brunch stop.

There are many, many more stops you can make along the St. Charles Line. Visit www.neworleansonline.com/tools/streets/saintcharles.html for a wonderful guide of things to do on your streetcar ride. If you catch the streetcar bug, you might want to ride the other lines such as the Riverfront Line, the Loyola Avenue Line, or the Canal Street Line, all with their own unique stops. So wherever you want to go, whatever you want to see, start with taking that first step onto a historic New Orleans streetcar!

ST. LOUIS CEMETERY
NO. 1 & NO. 2

BASIN ST. & CLAIBORNE AVE. • NEW ORLEANS, LA

(504) 596-3050 • SAVEOURCEMETERIES.ORG

Ever Seen "A City of the Dead"?

Tired of spending money and tipping waiters? In a city that depends on tourism, some activities are still free. One of these is roaming around the old cemeteries that border the French Quarter, named stoically St. Louis Cemetery No. 1 and St. Louis Cemetery No. 2. In the years following the founding of the city, death from disease, starvation, unsanitary conditions, and lethal retaliation was always near at hand and no one wanted to fool around with the grim reaper's sense of humor. Cemeteries were cemeteries and giving them flamboyant or inspiring names, such as found on streets or restaurants throughout the city, would not make them any less fearful. New Orleans is below sea level and the water table lurks just beneath the surface, so graves are above ground. Burial tombs, resembling miniature houses, are set on plots of land amid winding pathways, earning the morbid epithet, "Cities of the Dead." Rich families, civic and military associations, and benevolent organizations constructed whitewashed stucco mausoleums topped with barreled and gabled roofs.

The more famous or wealthier you were, the bigger your tomb and adornments. Vaults large enough to house multiple bodies feature marble statues, columns, or cryptic messages chiseled in stone. Crypts designed by famous architects and artists create an eerie labyrinth. In the early years, burial places were in high demand and spots in the larger vaults could be rented or sold to those needing a proper resting place for a loved one. This practice resulted in multiple,

Vintage Spot

MARIE LAVEAU TOMB: EST. 1881

No visit to St. Louis Cemetery No. 1 is complete without finding the tomb of Marie Laveau, voodoo priestess of old New Orleans, who refuses to leave the maze-like necropolis. The caramel-colored beauty learned herbal skills from her grandmother and cared for the wounded in the Battle of New Orleans. She dispensed indigenous herb potions, gris-gris charms, holy water, and incense to ease those suffering from malaria, yellow fever, tuberculosis, and dysentery. She reigned over voodoo rituals along Bayou St. John for nearly 50 years, gaining a reputation as a healer with divine powers.

It seems Laveau is buried in two separate tombs. The graves are eerily similar and both are marked with the iconic XXX, a code used if one wants to ask Laveau's spirit for favors. Both graves are decorated with Mardi Gras beads and other paraphernalia such as bananas, flowers, bones, bottles of rum, and signed notes. It's unsure which is "the" burial place of the high priestess. It is said that Laveau is alarmed by the vandalism of her tomb and haunts the cemetery day and night. Visitors have reported seeing the priestess in her signature seven-knot turban as she marches along the pathways reciting voodoo curses to rid her resting place of noisy tourists. Sometimes she morphs into a black cat with red eyes and Zombi, her 12-foot snake, occasionally comes out to bask atop her vault in the summer sun. Laveau doesn't like her tomb being vandalized, nor does she appreciate the rotting food left on her grave. But the rituals of Laveau devotees continue. How about you? Need a favor from the voodoo queen? A good fortune ritual is this: Turn around three times in front of Marie's tomb, knock three times to awaken her from the dead, mark the tomb with XXX in chalk, and then leave a gift. But beware: She doesn't like you doing this.

Basin St. & Claiborne Ave.;
(504) 596-3050; saveourcemeteries.org

unrelated names listed on crypt doors. Space in family vaults is still at a premium, and Louisiana law decrees that after 1 year and a day, coffins can be removed and the bagged bones of the deceased can either be pushed to the back of the vault or dropped into a holding area below, called a caveau, leaving room for another body on top.

St. Louis Cemetery No. 1 was first used as a burial place in 1789. By then St. Peter Cemetery in the French Quarter had nearly reached its capacity and city officials were anxious, in any case, to get the bodies from the latest yellow fever epidemic out of the city. You can sign on for one of the professional tours and learn a lot of history about the burial plots and those entombed within them. You can also saunter around on your own and discover for yourself some of the more famous gravesites. But be on your guard and heed the warning on the sign at the gated entrance that reads: "Visitors are welcome but enter these premises at their own risk. No security nor guards are provided and the New Orleans Archdiocesan cemeteries disclaims responsibility for the personal safety of visitors and their property."

Some well-known graves to look for are those of Etienne de Boré, the first mayor of New Orleans, and Ernest "Dutch" Morial, the first black mayor of the city who is the next-door neighbor of Marie Laveau, voodoo queen. One wonders what secrets these two are exchanging. You can also search for the memorial of Homer Plessy, plaintiff in the famous Supreme Court civil rights case, *Plessy v. Ferguson*. For fun, try to find the resting place of the French Creole playboy, Bernard de Marigny, who is credited with bringing the game of craps to the United States. Perhaps you can locate the grave of the elusive Barthelemy Lafon (he was one of Jean Lafitte's pirates). If you are a chess player, you might want to visit the gravesite of prodigy Paul Morphy, one of the earliest world chess champions, hailed as "the greatest player that ever lived."

People from all over the world are intrigued by this cemetery and the famous personages resting here. Some even wish to be in the in-crowd one day. Nicolas Cage, famous Hollywood actor, purchased a pyramid-shaped tomb as his final resting place. While most of the citizens of this cemetery are Catholic, others are welcomed . . . there is a small Protestant section in the northwestern sector. Before you leave this cemetery, you should know that it teems with paranormal activity, including EVPs (electronic voice phenomena), shadowy orbs, and apparitions. It is considered the most haunted cemetery in the world, and its picturesque decay has served as backdrops for films such as *Easy Rider* and *Interview with a Vampire*.

When you are finished strolling through St. Louis Cemetery No. 1, you can walk 3 blocks west toward Claiborne Avenue and take a look through St. Louis Cemetery No. 2, consecrated in 1823. Here you can find the grave of former Louisiana governor Arnaud Beauvois and Civil War brigadier general Pierre Buisson. If you are a music buff, you can search out the tombs of many musicians, such as Danny Barker and Ernie K. Doe of "Mother-in-Law" fame. Dominique You, another of Jean Lafitte's famous pirates, calls this place home. Ironically, one of his neighbors is the Venerable Mother Henriette DeLille, founder of the Sisters of the Holy Family "free women of color" religious order, who is presently up for canonization as a Roman Catholic saint.

Both cemeteries are listed on the US National Registry of Historic Places. If you are looking for a specific gravesite, you can go to Findagrave.com and search cemetery plots by name.

Here's a challenge for you. Can you find the grave of Delphine Lalaurie, the most hated woman in New Orleans in the mid 1800s?

ST. ROCH CEMETERY AND SHRINE

1725 ST. ROCH AVE. • NEW ORLEANS, LA 70117

(504) 945-5961 • NEWORLEANSONLINE.COM/DIRECTORY/

LOCATION.PHP?LOCATIONID=1953

Need a Cure for Tired Feet?

The St. Roch neighborhood is the heart of the Bywater District of New Orleans. This area lies just beyond the French Quarter and is one of the earliest developed areas outside the French Quarter due to the growth of New Orleans as a major port in the 19th century. Originally called Faubourg (a French term meaning suburb) Franklin, the neighborhood became popular in 1830 when the Pontchartrain Railroad connected nearby Faubourg Marigny to the settlement of Milneburg on the south shore of Lake Pontchartrain. It was an area of blacksmith shops, small farms and dairies, and local businesses. The area got its name from the St. Roch Shrine and Cemetery dedicated in 1876. Today you have a reason to visit the Bywater District, also known as the Upper Ninth Ward. The St. Roch Shrine and Mortuary Chapel are unique sights in a city that thrives on "different." Keep reading to find out why.

Back in the 1800s, yellow fever epidemics were the scourge of New Orleans. No one knew the cause of this horrific malaise, which did not discriminate as to its victims. Young and old, rich and poor, smart or dumb, everyone feared the fever and its probable deadly result. The families of wealthy citizens left the city when the weather turned warm, but businessmen had to stay behind and take their chances. Regular working class people and the poor could not escape at all. Thousands died in these epic yellow fever outbreaks.

A German priest, Rev. Peter Leonard Thevis, promised the Lord that if no one died in his Holy Trinity parish during the 1867 yellow fever epidemic, he would build a chapel to honor St. Roch, the patron saint of good health. The priest and his parishioners prayed, day and night, to St. Roch for protection. When none of his flock died in the horrible epidemic, Thevis honored his promise. Along with the chapel he also built a cemetery to provide a final resting place for his loyal parishioners. The shrine was designed in a simple but inspiring Gothic style and was completed in 1876.

To get to the St. Roch Shrine, you will have to drive or take a taxi. It's about a 15- to 20-minute ride from the French Quarter. The first thing you will notice is the beautiful name "Saint Roch's Campo Santo" (Italian for sacred field) made of elaborately twisted wrought iron just above the entrance gate. Take the time to look at the depictions of the stations of the cross, along the inside walls of the cemetery. It is said that women used to say the prayers of each station of the cross kneeling on the concrete. The small chapel is at the rear of the cemetery. Just walk down the center aisle. Enter the arched doorway and you can see a statue of St. Roch, also patron saint of dogs and dog lovers. A dog holding a loaf of bread in its mouth accompanies the statue of the saint. Reverend Thevis is buried beneath the floor in front of the altar.

Before you leave the chapel, take a few minutes to investigate the small alcove to the right of the entrance door. Many visitors to the chapel ask St. Roch for help with their disease or deformities in this tight space behind unlocked, easily opened iron bars. Here

Vintage Spot
ST. ROCH MARKET: EST. 1875

In the 19th century, public markets dotted the city landscape. The historic St. Roch Market dates back to 1875 when it was a vibrant part of old New Orleans. In its later years, the open-air market was known as a fish market that served some of the best gumbo and po'boys around, but the market struggled during the Depression and by the 1930s it was scheduled for demolition. Residents of the area rallied and held protests that resulted in the old brick-and-mortar building being given new life along with fully enclosed walls, refrigeration, and modern plumbing. The market was further improved in 1937 by the WPA program. After nearly 10 years of sitting vacant due to the devastating winds and floods of Hurricane Katrina, the St. Roch Market has reopened. Today the chain-link fence barrier has been removed and the moldering reminder of nature's wrath has been given a $3.7 million renovation. The market once again offers fresh local fruits and vegetables from multiple vendors and fresh-cut flowers from local urban growers. You can find lots of seafood choices, such as shrimp, crabs, and oysters, grab a salad and a cold-pressed juice from food vendors, or get a meal in the "neighborhood restaurant" in the rear of the market. For adventurous palates some new eateries offer alternatives to traditional New Orleans fare, such as the fusion of Korean and Creole cuisine offered by Koreole. There are multiple bar areas where you can get a beer, wine, or a cocktail to go with your oysters on the half shell doused with remoulade sauce.
2381 St. Claude Ave.; (504) 615-6541; strochmarket.com

you will see (you can also touch them, if you want to) mementos of cures attributed to St. Roch. Prosthetics, used plaster casts, replicas of body parts, crutches, and marble tiles saying "merci" or "thank-you" hang from the walls or lean against each other. People have left other things such as a burn victim's face mask and antique metal leg braces. The signs of gratitude, aka medical equipment, were no longer needed after the prayers of the faithful had been answered. Some visitors say it is all just a little creepy. One visitor said that her landlady sent her to the St. Roch shrine to leave a plastic ear as a prayer to help with her hearing. Among all this paraphernalia is a statue of a young woman known as St. Lucy, who was martyred by having her eyes plucked out. Her statue holds a plate of glass eyeballs in one hand.

Architecture buffs should take notice of the beautiful blue vaulted chapel ceiling with gilded adornments. Of special note are the gorgeous mosaics and statues throughout the cemetery. The shrine and mortuary chapel is open Monday through Friday from 8:30 a.m. to 4 p.m.

Hurricane Katrina was not the only blow to this struggling neighborhood, just the most recent. Back in the 1970s the interstate cut right through the heart of the Bywater District. The first phone number I remember when I lived with my mother and sister in a small duplex on Painters Street, just off Franklin Avenue, was a Bywater exchange, BY-3220. That childhood home was just one of many demolished to make way for progress. But today the area is coming back and is once again a vibrant place. Artists are discovering the eclectic neighborhood and its amenities. Many galleries are located within a few blocks of the St. Roch Shrine, so you can walk the cemetery, visit the chapel, and then go see some great local art.

STEAMBOAT *NATCHEZ* RIVERBOAT

TOULOUSE STREET WHARF (BEHIND JAX BREWERY, FRENCH
QUARTER) • NEW ORLEANS, LA 70130 • (504) 569-1401
STEAMBOATNATCHEZ.COM

If Mark Twain Could See You Now!

Mark Twain, the great American humorist and author of *Adventures of Huckleberry Finn* and *Life on the Mississippi*, was a riverboat pilot. He learned to navigate the mysterious and treacherous waters of the Mississippi River, which stretches more than 2,300 miles from its origins in Itasca Lake in Minnesota. The river winds its way right through the center of the country, forms parts of the boundaries of 10 states, and finally spills into the Gulf of Mexico, south of New Orleans.

When you climb aboard the *Natchez* for a relaxing 2-hour ride, you will feel as if you have entered another era. The captain barks his orders through an old-fashioned, hand-held megaphone while melodic strains emanate from the steam-driven calliope and the great paddlewheel churns the murky waters of the Mississippi River.

As the Natchez glides past the French Quarter, through one of the world's most active ports, you feel a part of history. The importance of the steamboat to New Orleans and the role it has played for almost two centuries must be explained.

In the 1820s, a booming population was moving west and the demand for goods to supply new towns and growing cities along the river was insatiable. The number of steamboats rose from 20 to 1,200 in a matter of years! Generally made of wood, the boats were designed either with a stern wheel or a side wheel that could churn through the muddy waters while only drawing up to 5 feet of water

even though they were loaded with cargo. Because of their flat-bottom design, steamboats were the most practical and cheapest way to move both goods and passengers along the river, which became quite shallow in some places. The power generated by their steam engines helped them navigate upriver against strong currents while loaded with bales of cotton, rice, timber, tobacco, molasses, and coal. The demand for more productivity meant an increase in the size of these boats. The earlier boats, 40 feet long and 10 feet wide, were soon overshadowed by some amazing steamboats stretching now to 300 feet long and 80 feet wide.

The first steamboat was called the *New Orleans*. Built in 1811, it ran between Natchez, Mississippi, and New Orleans, Louisiana, but very quickly, new steamboats such as the *Comet*, the *Vesuvius*, and the *Enterprise*, were navigating the river bends. The *Washington* was the first boat to have two decks, a lower deck for cargo and an upper deck for passengers.

The first steamboat to be named *Natchez*, built in 1823, plowed the river between New Orleans and Natchez. Its route was eventually expanded to reach from the Crescent City to Vicksburg, Mississippi. One of the most famous passengers of the first *Natchez* was the Marquis de Lafayette, of Revolutionary War fame. Unfortunately, the *Natchez* did not enjoy a long life; it was destroyed while in its New Orleans port by a fire on September 4, 1835.

Fire and boiler explosions were the two worst fears for steamboats during this early time and accounted for the destruction of some 500 vessels and over 4,000 lost lives. A boiler explosion on the *Sultana* near Memphis in 1865 took 1,800 lives, exceeding the number of lives lost on the Titanic. It is still considered the worst maritime disaster in US history. New federal regulations and building codes were introduced around this time to make river travel safer.

But it wasn't just commerce and passenger boats that thrived as part of life on the Mississippi. With more and more towns and states passing ordinances against gaming houses in town, the cheats moved to the unregulated waters of the Mississippi aboard river steamers. Gamblers seized on the opportunity to fleece would-be winners. Also, show folk saw the chance to entertain "captured" audiences, and new "showboats" began to travel up and down the mighty Mississippi. A showboat was a long, flat-roofed house positioned on a barge and pushed along by a small tugboat. The first showboat, named the *Floating Theatre*, was commissioned by William Chapman, a British-born actor in 1831. He and his family performed plays enhanced with music and dancing at various stops along the waterway. The boat left from Pittsburgh, Pennsylvania, and after reaching New Orleans, the boat was scuttled as it could not make the journey back against the river's current. The entertainers returned to Pittsburgh in a steamboat and readied their acts to perform again the next trip.

With the improvement of roads, the rise of the automobile, motion pictures, and the maturation of the river culture, cruise boats declined. They had a revival of sorts in the 1900s as they grew in size and became more elaborately designed with luxurious trappings for customer comfort. The *Cotton Blossom* and the *New Showboat* enticed famed jazzmen Louis Armstrong and Bix Biederbecke to climb aboard and play to sold-out crowds. In 1982 the *Natchez IX* won the Great Steamboat Race, as part of the Kentucky Derby Festival

held in Louisville. It has competed in five other races against the *Belle of Louisville*, the *Delta Queen*, the *Belle of Cincinnati*, the *American Queen*, and the *Mississippi Queen*, and has never lost!

The *Natchez* riverboat ride is a year-round popular treat for thousands of visitors, so check the website and plan your steamboat ride in advance. Cruising past the Chalmette Battlefield where the legendary Jean Lafitte joined forces with Andrew Jackson to defend the city at the Battle of New Orleans is inspiring, and the skyline of the Crescent City (especially in the evening) will take your breath away.

THE SUPERDOME

SUGAR BOWL DR. • NEW ORLEANS, LA 70112

(504) 587-3663 / (800) 756-7074 • MBSUPERDOME.COM

The Superdome Is Really SUPER!

*U*nless you are an avid architectural buff, you may not want to take a guided tour of the Superdome in New Orleans. But you have got to see this structure of magnificent proportions! So whether you fly over, drive by, or walk to it for a sporting or entertainment event, be ready to marvel in admiration at this architectural feat.

If you are familiar with the untraditional flair and intrigue of Louisiana politics, rest assured that building of the Superdome added to this notorious reputation! Originally the brainchild of Dave Dixon (who later founded the United States Football League), the idea of a superstructure came about as the lobbying efforts to bring an NFL team to the city bogged down in 1966. Commissioner Pete Rozelle said that New Orleans would never get awarded an NFL franchise without a domed stadium.

Dixon engaged the support of Governor John J. ("Big John") McKeithen, and the idea took shape while the governor was visiting the Astrodome in Houston, Texas. McKeithen reportedly said, "I want one of these, only bigger." Within months bonds were passed for the construction of the dome, and just 7 days later the NFL awarded the city its 25th professional football franchise. New Orleans named its team the Saints.

The plan was for the dome to be ready for the 1972 football season, at a construction tab of $46 million. But, due to political delays, construction did not begin until mid-year 1971, and disappointingly, was not finished in time for Super Bowl IX, which had been awarded

to the city for January 1975. It was too late for the game to be rescheduled to another city, and the Super Bowl was played at the un-domed Tulane Stadium in cold and rainy conditions.

When the Superdome was finally finished, the price tag had skyrocketed to $165 million. Despite this glitch, the huge domed stadium was an instant success, attracting sporting events such as the BCS National Championship Game (three times), five NCAA men's basketball Final Fours, and a record seven Super Bowl games.

Sporting events aside, the Superdome has attracted the attention of entertainment megastars. Sold-out concerts have broken previous attendance records due to the flexible seating capacity (73,000+) offered by the venue's versatile design. In 1981 the Rolling Stones packed the stadium to the rafters with 87,500 fans in what ranked as the world's largest indoor concert for over three decades. Frank Sinatra, Liza Minnelli, and Sammy Davis Jr. performed at the Superdome for the 1989 "The Ultimate Event" tour.

In 1995, the First Annual Essence Music Festival, the largest event celebrating African-American culture and music in the US, was held at the Superdome. It has been a huge attraction every year. In 2003 Stevie Wonder headlined the event, and in 2014 the festival

Vintage Spot

XAVIER UNIVERSITY OF LOUISIANA: EST. 1915

Xavier is the only Catholic, historically black university in the US. You can see the pale green rooflines and Xavier sign as you crest the bend on the elevated I-10 expressway into New Orleans. Xavier, founded by the Sisters of the Blessed Sacrament in 1915 as a high school, became a 4-year college in 1925. The college has grown considerably over the years, from five permanent buildings in 1948 to 16 today.

Dr. Norman C. Francis will retire in 2015 after 48 years at the helm. He is said to have been in office longer than any other university president to date. The university received a major endowment from the emirate of Qatar to build a pharmacy school as a part of the oil-rich country's outreach to the city after Hurricane Katrina in 2005. Today Xavier has one of only two accredited pharmacy programs in the state.

If you get the chance, stop by this grand institution and tour its historic campus.

1 Drexel Dr.; (504) 486-7411; xula.edu

celebrated its 20th anniversary with Prince as the main attraction. More than 50,000 tickets were sold to excited fans.

From music to boxing . . . Muhammad Ali regained his third world heavyweight title by defeating Leon Spinks in the Superdome in 1978. Another event of note was the famous "No Mas" fight between Sugar Ray Leonard and Roberto Duran, in which Duran turned to the referee in the eighth round and said "no more" in Spanish.

From boxing to basketball . . . in 1977, fans of "Pistol Pete" Maravich set an NBA attendance record of 35,077 as they watched the New Orleans Jazz play the Philadelphia 76ers, led by Julius Erving. Both Maravich and Erving were later inducted into the Basketball Hall of Fame.

From basketball to baseball, gymnastics, motocross, soccer, wrestling, the Republican National Convention, trade conventions of every imaginable type, and even the premiering of movies, the

Superdome has been a gracious host. In June 1996, *The Hunchback of Notre Dame*, Disney's 34th animated feature, was screened at the stadium with over 65,000 people in attendance.

Sitting on some 71 acres of land right in the middle of the city, the renamed Mercedes-Benz Superdome (2011) has been an awesome place of celebration, but it has been a scene of heartache too. As the world watched in horror, Hurricane Katrina ripped through this historic and charming city in the summer of 2005, eventually claiming the lives of over 1,800 people across four states and racking up $81 billion in damage. The Superdome was declared a "refuge of last resort" for the estimated 100,000 people still remaining and struggling for survival in the city. The dome had been built to withstand 200-mile-an-hour winds and flood levels up to 35 feet, but when Katrina hit, she ripped the "membrane" covering off the roof and two sections were compromised allowing water to flood inside. Despite this, the dome served as a safe haven for many of those stranded and in need. Within 7 months, all repairs to the Superdome were completed and the city rejoiced as their beloved New Orleans Saints defeated their archrival, the Atlanta Falcons, 23–3, before a sell-out crowd and a national TV audience. Hometown favorite Louisiana State University (LSU) came to town for Sugar Bowl festivities and beat Notre Dame, 41–14, the following January.

The Superdome is surrounded by its share of urban legends. Some fans believe the Saints have had many losing seasons because the dome was built on the site of what once was the Girod Street cemetery. Though the cemetery had been long abandoned, for many fans, the die was cast, and the spirits were angry! However, a miracle was at hand when the Saints won Super Bowl XLIV at the end of the 2009 season. Go figure!

Appendix A

PLACES BY CATEGORY

Activities—Playing, Sitting, Riding, Walking, or Marrying

French Quarter Wedding Chapel, 74
Rock 'n' Bowl, 157
The St. Charles Avenue Streetcar, 181
St. Louis Cemetery No. 1 & No. 2, 115, 184, 188
Steamboat *Natchez* Riverboat, 193
The Superdome, 198

Art

Rodrigue Studio, 160

Attractions

Audubon Zoo, 13
Blaine Kern's Mardi Gras World, 28
Jackson Square, 95
Old New Orleans Rum Distillery, 143

Bars

The Carousel Bar & Lounge, 43
Cats Meow, 47
Lafitte's Blacksmith Shop, 104
Mother-in-Law Lounge, 121
Old Absinthe House, 139
Pat O'Brien's, 151
Sazerac Bar & Grill, 172

Churches

Our Lady of Guadalupe Church, 148
St. Augustine Church, 116, 176
St. Roch Cemetery and Shrine, 189

Hotels

Andrew Jackson Hotel, 1

The Columns Hotel, 56

Hotel Monteleone, 44

Hotel Villa Convento, 83

The Roosevelt Hotel, 172

Museums

Audubon Butterfly Garden and
  Insectarium, 10

Backstreet Cultural Museum, 178

Beauregard-Keyes House, 24

La Pharmacie Française, 107

Louisiana's Civil War Museum, 117

Musée Conti Wax Museum, 128

National World War II
  Museum, 120

New Canal Lighthouse Museum
  & Education Center, 131

New Orleans Historic Voodoo
  Museum, 135

New Orleans Museum of Art, 54

New Orleans Pharmacy
  Museum, 108

Music Venues (live)

House of Blues, 87

Preservation Hall, 154

Parks

City Park, 50

Louis Armstrong Park, 113

Restaurants

Antoine's Restaurant, 5

Bud's Broiler, 37

Camellia Grill, 40

Commander's Palace, 60

The Court of Two Sisters, 65

Galatoire's Restaurant, 141

The Grocery, 79

Mother's, 124

Shops

Aunt Sally's, 19

Bourbon French Parfums, 32

The French Market, 69

Jackson Brewery Mall, 91

Rubensteins, 163

Theaters

Joy Theater, 100

Le Petit Théâtre du Vieux
Carré, 110

Mahalia Jackson Theater of the
Performing Arts, 115

Saenger Theatre, 168

Appendix B

PLACES BY NEIGHBORHOOD

Canal Street

Audubon Butterfly Garden and
Insectarium, 10
Joy Theater, 100

Rubensteins, 163
Saenger Theatre, 168
Sazerac Bar & Grill, 172

Carrollton

Camellia Grill, 40

Rock 'n' Bowl, 157

City Park

City Park, 50

Bud's Broiler (seven
locations), 37

Frenchmen Street

Old New Orleans Rum
Distillery, 143

St. Roch Cemetery and
Shrine, 189

French Quarter

Andrew Jackson Hotel, 1
Antoine's Restaurant, 5
Aunt Sally's, 19
Beauregard-Keyes House, 24
Bourbon French Parfums, 32
The Carousel Bar & Lounge, 43
Cats Meow, 47
The Court of Two Sisters, 65
The French Market, 69

French Quarter Wedding
Chapel, 74
Hotel Villa Convento, 83
House of Blues, 87
Jackson Square, 95
Lafitte's Blacksmith Shop, 104
La Pharmacie Française, 107
Le Petit Théâtre du Vieux
Carré, 110

Musée Conti Wax Museum, 128
Old Absinthe House, 139
Pat O'Brien's, 151
Preservation Hall, 154

New Orleans Historic Voodoo
   Museum, 135
Rodrigue Studio, 160

Garden District

Audubon Zoo, 13
The Columns Hotel , 56
Commander's Palace, 60

The Grocery, 79
The St. Charles Avenue
   Streetcar, 181

Just outside the French Quarter

Louis Armstrong Park, 113
Mother-in-Law Lounge, 121
Our Lady of Guadalupe
   Church, 148

St. Augustine Church, 116, 176
St. Louis Cemetery No. 1 & No. 2,
   115, 184, 188

Lakefront

New Canal Lighthouse Museum
   & Education Center, 131

Lee's Circle

Louisiana's Civil War Museum, 117

Mississippi River

Blaine Kern's Mardi Gras
   World, 28
Jackson Brewery Mall, 91

Steamboat *Natchez*
   Riverboat, 193

Poydras

Mother's, 124
The Superdome, 198

Appendix C

PLACES BY YEAR OF ORIGIN

1700s: Andrew Jackson Hotel, 1

1720s: The French Market, 69

1789: St. Louis Cemetery No. 1 & No. 2, 184

1807: Old Absinthe House, 139

1815: Jackson Square (in 1700s Place d'Armes), 95

1826: Beauregard-Keyes House, 24

1826: Our Lady of Guadalupe Church, 148

1831: (horse-drawn; 1890s electric) The St. Charles Avenue Streetcar, 181

1832: The Court of Two Sisters, 65

1839: New Canal Lighthouse Museum & Education Center, 131

1840: Antoine's Restaurant, 5

1842: St. Augustine Church, 176

1843: Bourbon French Parfums, 32

1850s: City Park, 50

1876: St. Roch Cemetery and Shrine, 189

1880: Commander's Palace, 60

1884: Audubon Zoo, 13

1886: The Carousel Bar & Lounge, 43

1891: Louisiana's Civil War Museum, 117

1922: Le Petit Théâtre du Vieux Carré (in 1794 town house), 110

1924: Rubensteins, 163

1929: Saenger Theatre, 168

1933: Lafitte's Blacksmith Shop (in 1772 blacksmith shop), 104

1935: Aunt Sally's, 19

1938: Mother's, 124

1940s: Rock 'n' Bowl (moved in 2009), 157

1942: Pat O'Brien's (in 1791 building), 151

1946: Camellia Grill, 40

1946: Joy Theater, 100

1947: Blaine Kern's Mardi Gras World, 28

1949: Sazerac Bar & Grill (in 1893 hotel), 172

1950: La Pharmacie Française (in 1823 pharmacy), 107

1952: Bud's Broiler, 37

1961: Preservation Hall (in 1750 building), 154

1964: Musée Conti Wax Museum (in 1890 town house), 128

1972: New Orleans Historic Voodoo Museum, 135

1975: Steamboat *Natchez* Riverboat (with 1925 steering system), 193

1975: The Superdome, 198

1980: Louis Armstrong Park (in 1800s Congo Square), 113

1980: The Columns Hotel (in 1883 mansion), 56

1981: Hotel Villa Convento (in 1833 town house), 83

1984: Jackson Brewery Mall (in 1890 brewery), 91

1989: Cats Meow (in 1820s town house), 47

1994: House of Blues, 87

1994: Mother-in-Law Lounge, 121

1995: Old New Orleans Rum Distillery (in 1800s cotton warehouse), 143

1999: French Quarter Wedding Chapel, 74

2003: The Grocery (in 1800s building), 79

2008: Audubon Butterfly Garden and Insectarium (in 1848 Custom House), 10

2010: Rodrigue Studio (in 1800s town house), 160

Bibliography

American Bicycle Rental Company website. www.bikerentalnew orleans.com (accessed December 6, 2014).

Aunt Sally's website. www.auntsallys.com (accessed February 5, 2015).

Bourbon French Parfums website. www.neworleansperfume.com (accessed January 10, 2015).

Cats Meow website. www.catskaraoke.com (accessed January 7, 2015).

Cipra, David L. *Lighthouses, Lightships, and the Gulf of Mexico.* Alexandria, VA: Cypress Communications, 1997.

The Court of Two Sisters website. www.courtoftwosisters.com (accessed December 15, 2014).

Dorrance, Laurel A. "Dufilho, Grandchamps, or Peyroux? The Development of Professional Pharmacy in Colonial and Early National American Louisiana" (2011), University of New Orleans Theses and Dissertations, Paper 1305, scholarworks.uno.edu/td (accessed September 21, 2014).

Dwyer, Jeff. *Ghost Hunter's Guide to New Orleans.* Gretna, LA: Pelican Publishing Company, 2007.

Fraiser, Jim. *The French Quarter of New Orleans.* Jackson: University Press of Mississippi, 2003.

Franko, Vanessa. "COACHELLA 2014: Preservation Hall Jazz Band Seasons Indio with New Orleans Flavor," *The Press-Enterprise*, April 16, 2014, pe.com/articles/band-693103-jazz-preservation .html (accessed October 19, 2014).

French Quarter Wedding Chapel website. www.frenchquarter weddingchapel.com (accessed October 19, 2014).

Garbarino, Steve. "Iconic Rubensteins Celebrates 90 Years as N.O. Trendsetter." *The Advocate.* Special to *The Advocate*. April 08, 2014. http://theadvocate.com/news/neworleans/new orleansnews/8797858-123/rubensteins-celebrates-90-years-as (accessed March 17, 2014).

The Historic New Orleans Collection Quarterly. Acquisitions: Vol. 27, No. 3, Summer 2010. hnoc.org/publications/galleries/quarterly/pdf/HNOC_Q3_10.pdf (accessed December 14, 2014).

House of Blues website. www.houseofblues.com/neworleans (accessed November 16, 2014).

Joy Theater website. www.thejoytheater.com (accessed November 5, 2014).

Klein, Victor C. *New Orleans Ghosts.* Chapel Hill, NC: Lycanthrope Press, 1993.

Krane, Jim. "The Octoroon Mistress," Nola.com, March 7, 1998, nola.com/haunted/ghosts/octoroon.html (accessed November 11, 2014).

Laufer, Geraldine Adamich. "History of the Apothecary: The New Orleans Pharmacy Museum," *The Herb Companion*, herbcompanion.com/Health/Old-Time-Apothecary.aspx (accessed December 14, 2014).

McNulty, Ian. "Candy Maker Expands, but Keeps an Eye on Its Roots." *The Advocate* www.theneworleansadvocate.com/features/7812863-171/creole-candy-maker-expands-but (accessed March 17, 2015).

Musée Conti Wax Museum website. www.neworleanswaxmuseum.com (accessed December 21, 2014).

My House Nola. "Drink Up: Old New Orleans Rum." http://nolavie.com/drink-up-old-new-orleans-rum-24339/ (accessed March 17, 2015).

New Orleans Historic Voodoo Museum website. www.artcom.com/Museums/vs/mr/70116-31.htm (accessed March 17, 2015).

Pat O'Brien's website. www.patobriens.com (accessed March 17, 2015).

Preservation Hall website. www.preservationhall.com (accessed December 18, 2014).

Rodrigue, George. *Foundation of the Arts*, Biography and Timeline. georgerodriguefoundation.org/site372.php (accessed November 6, 2014).

Spera, Keith. "Rock 'n' Bowl Felt Like Home, Even in a Shiny New Space," NOLA.com. *Times-Picayune*, Posted on 4/16/2009, blog.nola.com/keithspera/2009/04/rock_n_bowl_felt_like_home_eve.html (accessed December 4, 2014).

———. "Watch: Rock 'n' Bowl Murals Move to Their New Home."
NOLA.com, *Times-Picayune*, Posted on 6/2/2009, blog.nola.com/
keithspera/2009/06/what_about_the_murals_as.html (accessed
December 4, 2014).

Stuart, Bonnye E. *Haunted New Orleans*. Guilford, CT: Globe Pequot
Press, 2012.

———. *Louisiana Curiosities*. Guilford, CT: Globe Pequot Press, 2012.

Tucker, Abigail. "The New Orleans Historic Voodoo Museum,"
Smithsonian Magazine, June 2011, smithsonianmag.com/
arts-culture/the-new-orleans-historic-voodoo-museum
-160505840/?no-ist (accessed January 6, 2015).

Turner, Richard Brent. *Jazz Religion, the Second Line, and Black New
Orleans*. Bloomington: Indiana University Press, 2009.

Walenter, Katie. "Aunt Sally's Pralines," *Gambit*, BestofNewOrleans
.com, bestofneworleans.com/gambit/aunt-sallys-pralines/
Content?oid=2485227 (accessed December 12, 2014).

Index

A

American Bicycle Rental
 Company, 77
Andrew Jackson Hotel, 1
Antoine's Restaurant, 5
Audubon Butterfly Garden and
 Insectarium, 10
Audubon Park, 10
Audubon Zoo, 13
Aunt Sally's, 19

B

Backstreet Cultural
 Museum, 178
Beauregard-Keyes House, 24
Beauregard, Pierre Gustave
 Toutant, 24
Blaine Kern's Mardi Gras
 World, 28
Botanical Garden and
 Conservatory, 53
Bourbon French Parfums, 32
Bud's Broiler, 37
Bywater District, 189

C

Cabildo, The, 99
Camellia Grill, 40
Canal Street, 100
Carousel Bar & Lounge, The, 43
Cats Meow, 47

City Park, 50
Columns Hotel, The, 56
Commander's Palace, 60
Congo Square, 113
cornstalk fence, 4, 58
Court of Two Sisters, The, 65
Couturie Forest, 53

D

Dueling Oak, 52
Dufilho, Louis Joseph, Jr., 107
Dupas, Dr. James, 107

F

Faubourg Marigny, 178
Feelings Café, 71
French Market, The, 69
French Quarter Wedding
 Chapel, 74

G

Galatoire's Restaurant, 141
Gandolfo, Charles Massicot, 136
Garden District, the, 56, 60, 79,
 181, 182
Grocery, The, 79

H

Hansen's Sno-Bliz and
 Sweetshop, 82
Hotel Monteleone, 44

Hotel Villa Convento, 83
House of Blues, 87

J
Jackson Brewery Mall, 91
Jackson Square, 95
Joy Theater, 100

K
K-Doe, Ernie, 121
Kern, Blaine, 28
Keyes, Frances Parkinson, 24

L
Lafayette Cemetery No. 1, 62
Lafayette, City of, 60
Lafitte, Jean, 104, 139
Lafitte's Blacksmith Shop, 104
Lake Pontchartrain, 131
La Pharmacie Française, 107
Laveau, Marie, 186
Le Petit Théâtre du Vieux
    Carré, 110
Louis Armstrong Park, 113
Louisiana's Civil War
    Museum, 117

M
Mahalia Jackson Theater of the
    Performing Arts, 115
Marie Laveau Tomb, 186
Mercedes-Benz
    Superdome, 198
Meyer the Hatter, 165
Monkey Hill, 15
Moon Walk, 97
Mother-in-Law Lounge, 121
Mother's, 124

M.S. Rau Antiques, 35
Mullen, Wilhelmina, 160
Musée Conti Wax Museum, 128

N
National World War II Museum,
    117, 120
New Canal Lighthouse Museum
    & Education Center, 131
New Orleans Historic Voodoo
    Museum, 135
New Orleans Museum of
    Art, 54
New Orleans Pharmacy
    Museum, 108
NOLA Brewery, 93

O
Old Absinthe House, 139
Old New Orleans Rum
    Distillery, 143
Our Lady of Guadalupe
    Church, 148

P
Pat O'Brien's, 151
Pigeontown, 40
Preservation Hall, 154
P-town, 40

R
Rock 'n' Bowl, 157
Rodrigue, George, 160
Rodrigue Studio, 160
Roosevelt Hotel, The, 172
Rubenstein, Morris, 163
Rubensteins, 163

S

Saenger Theatre, 168
Saint Expedite, 150
Sazerac Bar & Grill, 172
Short, Col. Robert Henry, 58
Spotted Cat Music Club, 145
St. Augustine Church, 116, 176
St. Charles Avenue Streetcar,
    The, 181
St. Louis Cemetery No. 1,
    115, 184
St. Louis Cemetery No. 2, 188
St. Roch Cemetery and
    Shrine, 189
St. Roch Market, 191
Steamboat *Natchez*
    Riverboat, 193

Superdome, The, 198

T

Tad Gormley Stadium, 53
Tremé, 113

U

Upper Ninth Ward, 189
US Custom House, 11

V

Vieux Carré, 74

X

Xavier University of
    Louisiana, 200